THE MAGIC OF
PRAYER

An Introduction to the Psychology of Faith

M.D. FABER

PRAEGER

Westport, Connecticut
London

Library of Congress Cataloging-in-Publication Data

Faber, M.D. (Mel D.)
    The magic of prayer : an introduction to the psychology of faith / M.D. Faber.
      p. cm.
    Includes bibliographical references and index.
    ISBN 0–275–97385–9 (alk. paper)
      1. Psychology, Religious. 2. Prayer—Psychology. I. Title.
    BL51.F29 2002
    291.4′2—dc21   2001032913

British Library Cataloguing in Publication Data is available.

Library of Congress Catalog Card Number: 2001032913
ISBN: 0–275–97385–9

First published in 2002

Praeger Publishers, 88 Post Road West, Westport, CT 06881
An imprint of Greenwood Publishing Group, Inc.
www.praeger.com

Printed in the United States of America

The paper used in this book complies with the
Permanent Paper Standard issued by the National
Information Standards Organization (Z39.48–1984).

10 9 8 7 6 5 4 3 2 1

This book is dedicated to
the memory of my brother,
Stuart Michael Faber

CONTENTS

PREFACE

I came to this book in a circuitous fashion. For several years I had been concentrating intensively upon New Age thinking, upon what I regard in my own mind as the retreat into magic in an age of science. I had devoted three lengthy discussions to shamanism, channeling, witchcraft, crystals, psychic healing, synchronicity, and to the New Age version of the cosmos, the attempt on the part of New Agers to transform an unfathomable, mysterious, perhaps infinite universe of colossal forces into a cozy psychic home for the spiritually homeless. As I went about my business, I frequently discovered mainstream religious writers (Catholic, Protestant, and Jewish) attacking New Age thinking for its reliance upon magical beliefs and behaviors. In this newspaper, in that anthology, in this magazine, on that television show, the traditional religionists decried what they perceived (correctly) to be a genuine absorption in necromancy on the part of numerous, apparently grown-up and intelligent people. This intrigued me. Although I had always known that religion abhorred magic, I was also accustomed in my thoughts to joining religion and magic in some significant yet unspecified way. Were not religious beliefs and practices, religious texts and rituals, everywhere streaked with strikingly magical elements: seas parting, people turning into pillars of salt, prophets conversing with spirits, frogs raining down from the skies, statues bleeding, wine becoming blood, bread becoming flesh, the dead awakening? How could such items fail to bring magic to mind?

When my interest in New Age thinking subsided, I turned my attention to the vast realm of religion, and soon found myself engrossed in William James's great book, *The Varieties of Religious Experience*. There, I learned that supplication was the central religious behavior and the *sine qua non* of religious faith. To pray—and I mean sincerely—was to have a religious life of some kind; to cease praying altogether was to become religiously dormant, or dead. I also learned that for James both the emotional benefits of prayer and the powerful sense of reality that often accompanied prayer, the sense that something or someone was present, was there, were best explained through reliance upon the supernatural sphere, upon what James called transmundane energies, and finally, toward the close of his book, God. I had the feeling as I read that James was struggling mightily, perhaps heroically, with this and reaching his conclusions almost in spite of himself. Yet there they were. Inspired by this wonderful volume, I went on to explore in earnest the literature of supplication. If religion had something to tell me about magic, and magic about religion, it would probably emerge, I now recognized, through an in-depth, energetic probing of supplicatory conduct.

By the time I had completed this task, two major realizations were well established within me: first, I realized that prayer itself was magical behavior, not in some loose, informal sense, but in the rigorous sense that pervaded the professional anthropological literature. Although supplication lacked the willfulness, the stridency, that characterized the magical actions of New Agers, although it struck a different attitude, evinced a different quality, it nevertheless fell into the realm of magical conduct, at least as magical conduct was understood by those who had dealt with it illustriously over the past two hundred years. Second, I realized that in setting this forth I would be offering the reader not merely an explanation of prayer but a naturalistic alternative to the supernaturalism of James's pivotal book. Where James found transmundane energies, or God, at work in supplication, I found only human fantasy and longing. Even the strong sense of reality that accompanied prayer, the sense of something being there, indeed that most of all, could be thoroughly and convincingly interpreted along naturalistic, psychological lines. While prayer was certainly mysterious and difficult to fathom, it did not require us, ultimately, to resort to explanations beyond, or outside of, the natural order of things. I use the word *alternative* for obvious reasons. The existence of God and the nature of prayer are not items that can be established or refuted in a manner that reflects our current empirical understanding of proof. We cannot demonstrate the existence of God as we demonstrate the existence of, for example, an electron; we cannot get at the nature of prayer as we get at the nature of, for example, table salt. We can only offer our views as lucidly, as logically, as forcefully as possible and leave it to readers to make their decision, their choice.

Because prayer is so vast a topic, I decided to limit myself to individual, subjective prayer in the Judeo–Christian tradition (on two or three occasions I refer to Islam). Because prayer is so sensitive a topic, because supplication is so precious to those who practice it, I recognized from the outset the inevitability of creating a controversial study. There is just no way to present prayer along naturalistic, psychological lines without irritating someone, or even chafing someone's feelings. Permit me to say the following on this score: although I am not inclined to pussyfoot around, I am also not inclined to be disrespectful or cruel. I came to my conclusions honestly, candidly, and also painstakingly in the light of my theoretical assumptions. Like James, I saw no alternative to those conclusions. They were to me the only believable way to go and therefore the only honorable way to go. Finally, I very much doubt that those who pray will feel prone to stop after reading this book. At the same time, they may well find themselves with some fresh thoughts about prayer, and from my educative, pedagogical angle, that's good. As for those who don't pray, they are not likely to begin as they put this volume down; but then, one never knows. The Lord, as the old expression has it, works in mysterious ways.

CHAPTER 1

INTRODUCTION: ALTERNATIVE VARIETIES OF RELIGIOUS EXPERIENCE

NATURALISM AND SUPERNATURALISM: ALTERNATIVE APPROACHES

Toward the close of his enlightened treatise *The Varieties of Religious Experience* ([1902] 1987), William James addresses directly the truth-claims of religion. How are we to regard the remarkable materials that inform the book as a whole: the mystical interludes, the enraptured visions, the passionate expressions of faith, the tangible benefits of prayer, including physical healing, spiritual transformation, and the alleviation of anxiety and grief? Is there anything objective about all this, asks James (455)? Is there a supernatural realm with which humans are somehow in contact, a realm that explains, in some manner or measure, the nature of religious experience? Although he knows that "the current of thought in academic circles runs against" him, although he realizes what he is about to say will be "shocking to the reigning intellectual tastes" (466), James goes ahead and lays it on the line: "I believe that a candid consideration of piecemeal supernaturalism and a complete discussion of all its metaphysical bearings will show it to be the hypothesis by which the largest number of legitimate requirements [for a plausible explanation] are met" (466). He continues:

> I have no hypothesis to offer beyond what the phenomenon of "prayerful communion," especially when certain kinds of incursion from the subconscious region take part in it, immediately suggests. The appearance is that in this phenomenon something ideal, which in

one sense is part of ourselves and in another sense is not ourselves, actually exerts an influence, raises our centre of personal energy, and produces regenerative effects unattainable in other ways. (467)

And finally,

If, then, there be a wider world of being than that of our every-day consciousness, if in it there be forces whose effects on us are intermittent, if one facilitating condition of the effects be the openness of the "subliminal" door, we have the elements of a theory to which the phenomena of religious life lend plausibility . . . At these places at least, I say, it would seem as though transmundane energies, God, if you will, produced immediate effects within the natural world to which the rest of our experience belongs. (467)

Their sophisticated language aside, James's conclusions are congruent with the views of believers everywhere, with the "piecemeal supernaturalism" of the religious community worldwide. God exists and in some mysterious way is present in our lives. It is precisely the "phenomenon" of "prayerful communion"—for James, "the very soul and essence of religion" (416)—that attests most vividly, most "energetically" as it were, to the reality of His presence. The individual who prays sincerely, who manages to access his deepest feelings, the "subconscious region" itself, may very well discover his own personal link to the Divine.

I begin this way because James's remarks help me to focus my purpose here. Employing my own mix of examples and ideas, my own combination of data and hypotheses, I mean to develop an exclusively naturalistic account of religious experience and offer it to the reader as an alternative to the supernaturalism of the religious world in general and of James's book in particular. Naturalism is defined as a theory denying that an object or event has a supernatural significance and suggesting that scientific laws are adequate to account for all phenomena. More specifically, I intend to concentrate on "prayerful communion" in a manner that will render superfluous, or perhaps otiose, the "transmundane energies, God, if you will," upon which James and the religious community ultimately depend. I am not suggesting in the previous three sentences, of course, that I plan to explain the whole of religious experience, both past and present, as it has flourished in the world. Indeed, religious experience—and by that I mean the intense, subjective, "subconscious" kind on which James concentrates in his book—is so variegated, so ancient, so "boundless," in a word, that only a madman would set out to explain the whole of it. My intention is simply to offer enough to fashion a reasonably thorough and coherent view, one that discloses, if not everything, then a number of crucial, central features, the proverbial "pith" of the matter.

I present what I am doing as an alternative to supernaturalism, or "God, if you will," because religious experience as James describes it cannot be subjected to "hard" or "rigorous" analysis in the manner in which we usually employ those terms—a point of which James was fully aware. We are dealing, truth told, with subjective states, with emotions, with what psychoanalytic psychology calls "affect" in its effort to wed unconscious developmental factors from the past to the individual's current feelings or inclinations. The materials that arise from this non-Cartesian world of perceptual, mind-body experience will be of necessity "soft," or elusive, both in relation to our examples and the conclusions we draw from them. The person who attempts to prove (or disprove) the naturalistic nature of religious experience in a manner similar to that which he would use to prove (or disprove) the heliocentric theory of the solar system or the molecular theory of chemical bonding will fall flat on his face. This does not mean that I won't try to establish my argument in a powerful, utterly convincing way. It does not mean that I won't proceed as if I had the answers, as if I were laying the matter bare, for every intelligent individual to see. Quite the contrary, I'll strive to build an airtight case. At the same time, I realize that supernaturalists everywhere are just as convinced of their views as I am of mine. When the dust settles, the reader will simply make up his mind as to which explanation is more credible, the naturalistic or the supernaturalistic one, as I present them of course.

My success here depends overwhelmingly on what we can think of as fine-grained work. Again and again I will subject my quotations, my examples, my data from the religious realm to intense, close, even delicate probing along specific theoretical lines set forth in chapter 2, where I offer the reader a psychodynamic model of human development with special emphasis on the first years of life, the years during which the seeds of religious belief are sown. Ultimately I am looking for connections between religious belief as it emerges through narrative, precept, metaphor, and symbol, and psychological proposition as it emerges through clinical, therapeutic practice and through related anthropological study of magical behavior. From the meticulous, fine-grained application of analytical insight to religious expression, and from this alone, the meaning of the book will emanate. To put the matter another way, the book depends entirely on the reader being struck by the details of the analysis, by the unmistakable, even amazing correspondences between the religious and the psychological materials I bring to bear. This must occur many times, over scores of pages, until the argument in all its complexity is finally established. As for the book's overall thesis, or contention, it can be rendered thus: individual, subjective prayer, the kind we discover in James, is finally an instance of homeopathic magical conduct. It conjures up ritualistically a version of the first, primal, biological situation in which the dependent little one cries out to the parental big one for physical and emotional nourishment.

The very instructional details of individual prayer are unconsciously designed to recreate the magical alliance in and through which our existence on the planet commences and goes forward. Over and over again, dozens of times each day, hundreds of times each week, thousands of times each month, each year, the little one asks and the big one sees to it that the little one receives. (The key biblical injunction for prayer is, ask and ye shall receive [Mark 11:24].) Such asking and receiving is the central feature, the very essence, of the child's reality, or world. As the developing child comes to internalize this persistent, endless conditioning, to set it up as the inward scaffolding of his psychological life (hope and trust, the legacy of the good, internalized object), he comes to dwell within an inner psychic universe of compelling, unseen, providential presences (his emergent feelings and voices, his transferential associations to the object). When he is subsequently introduced to the supernatural realm through cultural experience (God, the angels), he takes to it naturally, readily, because in a manner of speaking he has been there all along. He knows all about compelling, invisible presences. Moreover, he wants to perpetuate, to continue, the nourishing relation on which his existence has thus far been based. Thus religious belief, religious conviction, or faith as it comes through prayer, is a species of the uncanny. The practitioner is unconsciously or psychically returned to the parental alliance which he knew and enjoyed in the beginning and which he now complexifies and elaborates in accordance with his current requirements and the promptings of culture (scripture, theology, precept, artifact). The early biological arrangement is transformed into a practical, magical alliance with an omnipotent supernatural being, an alliance that can be used on a daily basis, just as the original alliance was used. The universal theological precept that prayer leads to faith and that faith manifests itself in prayer might be thought of as the magical circle of religious belief. So vital, so dynamic, so life-sustaining and precious is our first biological attachment to the caregiver, so deeply are we conditioned as little ones into believing that this arrangement is reality, the world, the universe, that we simply (and perhaps wisely) refuse to relinquish it. We want to separate and grow up, yet we do not want to separate and grow up. From precisely this developmental crisis (which is ongoing throughout the course of the life cycle) springs our religious belief and behavior, our method of achieving separation and remaining tied to the matrix, all in the same psychological moment—in a word, our method of playing it both ways.

The creative magic of religion is devoted largely to addressing this rooted human dilemma, including of course the dilemma of death, the final separation. We often associate magic with sleight of hand. We might well think of religious magic generally as humankind's collective and virtually impenetrable sleight of mind. There it is. The reader now has the book's thesis, the bits of information that say everything. For many readers this will be sufficient. What more is required, after all, in an informational age, an age of bits and bytes, of items popping up on colored monitors? Other readers, by contrast, will appreciate that up to exactly this point in the discussion very little has been said. For these readers the essential discourse is yet to come; the actual voyage, as it were, is yet to commence, and that includes the intellectual tension and excitement that may attend fine-grained work. To the first group of readers, I say *adios amigos*; it is time for you to move on to another book. To the second group, I say welcome aboard; I'll do my best to make the trip both enjoyable and—yes, of course—informative.

I want also to make plain at this juncture my disagreement with those who subscribe to either or both of the related notions that (1) only theologians and philosophers, as opposed to psychologists, may rightfully evaluate religion's truth-claims, and that (2) only "insiders," or actual members of actual sects, are in a position to understand the rituals and beliefs of religious denominations. These notions are easily discovered in the literature, so frequently do they turn up. "The task of assessing the truth-claims of religion belongs to theology or philosophy, not to psychology," declares Hinnells's *Dictionary of Religions* (1995, 394), characterizing this view. In another passage of the *Dictionary* (500) we find, "religion(s) cannot be studied successfully by one who is not a religious practitioner." But surely religious beliefs and behaviors are a major, integral expression of our basic human nature, our primal quality as people. To exclude psychology from a central feature of religion, namely the assertion of and the subscription to truth-claims, to maintain that psychologists have no business evaluating or assessing the validity of such things, strikes me as not only futile but bizarrely elitist and defensive as well. If, for example, the members of a particular sect hold that peaches, when addressed with certain sacred syllables uttered by certain sacred individuals, become sanctified and harbor within their flesh the spirit of an omnipotent deity, then surely I as a psychologist may offer my assessment of what that means as a truth-claim, in the light of my psychological (and naturalistic) assumptions about human behavior, of course. Moreover, why are philosophers and theologians in a better position than me to assess the nature and/or the accuracy of truth-claims? Do not they come to the table bearing their own assumptions and outlooks? If we are all loaded up in this postmodern age with our cultural biases and contextual presuppositions, if we all labor away within the hermeneutic circle of our inescapable backgrounds and rooted opinions, then let's simply get on with it, keeping the limitations and imperfections in mind, and asserting our objections and/or agreements in the appropriate ways and places.

Let's simply thrash things out as tainted equals in the free and open marketplace of ideas. I can understand that psychologists may well annoy the religious by analyzing their cherished beliefs and practices, but surely psychologists have every intellectual right in the world to do so. If the religious consider such analyses to be misguided, or purblind, then so be it; but religion, whether it likes it or not, must take its place among the institutions of humanity and be studied accordingly, and that includes its truth-claims. It cannot, without incurring grave danger to its long-term survival, wall itself off in the medieval cathedrals of the mind. Very much the same may be said for the notion that only insiders, or *aficionados* if I may be allowed, can truly appreciate the significance and the quality of a particular creed or system of belief. Indeed, it is often the insiders who are in the worst position to perceive matters clearly and to assess them with insight, so shaped are they by the socialization, even the conditioning, that generally produces insiders in the first place. One need look no further than the nearest cult, or crusade, or revival tent to get my meaning here.

Of course we must be very, very sensitive to the inward, life-sustaining nature of religious creeds and specific truth-claims. Of course we must appreciate that psychological analysis frequently impinges on truth-claim by its very nature. To say what something means psychologically is to imply where it resides epistemically. When psychologists maintain that "God" is a projection of the human mind—an everyday occurrence in psychological circles—they call into question, or assess negatively, every religious truth-claim in the history of the world, without exception. And of course we must try hard to put ourselves in the psychic skin of the believer and to apprehend the world through his eyes rather than through our own. If we fail to do these things, we will probably also fail to produce an analysis of value to either the religionist or the psychologist. To declare, however, that we cannot as psychologists legitimately assess truth-claims or know anything of significance from the outside is ultimately to declare that religion is and must remain unanalyzable—as naturalism in particular understands analysis. It is to beat the drum vigorously for a monadic religious universe in which only the privileged may speak and in which everyone else must shut up. Obviously, I won't be marching to that beat in what follows.

Nor will I be justifying anything in what James ([1902] 1987, 26) calls "empiricist" terms. I allude to his famous *mot* that religious practices do not work because they are true, but are true because they work. James writes, "not its origin, but *the way in which it works on the whole*, is [the] final test of a belief. This is our . . . empiricist criterion; and this criterion the stoutest insisters on supernatural origin have also been forced to use in the end. . . . By their fruits ye shall know them, not by their roots" (26). My tripartite response to this arises, of course, from my vastly differing outlook on the entire matter, an outlook based firmly on psychoanalytic psychology. I am interested primarily in roots, not fruits, in questions of the nature, or the quality, of religious experience exactly as such questions relate to psychological origins. Not only do I mean to probe from a naturalistic, developmental angle whence the supernatural springs, or how it arises in the human mind, but I also mean to suggest what that signifies for, or what that says about, religious experience as a facet of human experience and human potential as a whole. As we have seen, James concludes toward the end of his wonderful book that the supernatural probably exists and probably explains something about religion's fruits (and also about its roots, as it happens). By contrast, I will suggest, and hopefully demonstrate in the fine-grained work that follows—and especially in chapter 3—that the supernatural is a human fabrication with no basis in reality, that it is grounded entirely in human subjectivity, in the largely unconscious inclination to diminish anxiety and increase emotional security, thereby alleviating the stress inherent in our situation on the planet. In this way, the roots come first for me because the roots as they are analyzed and disclosed help us to resolve the old, fascinating issues traditionally associated with the religious realm: Does "God, if you will" exist? What is the nature and meaning of religious experience? Why is religion there, to begin with? Why do millions of people turn to it? What are we as humans doing when we behave religiously?

Again (and second), the argument from fruits as opposed to roots is really no argument at all; it has no substance in discursive, rational, philosophic terms, no bite. Nothing is analyzed or debated; nothing is established by way of logical reasoning, or proof. The argument from fruits is simply an observation and a rather obvious one at that: religion helps. Well, in many instances and in manifold ways, it may; but religion does have its dark side too, its history of persecution and dementia, of tyranny and bloodshed. In fairness to James (and to get this burden off my own shoulders), *The Varieties of Religious Experience* deals primarily with powerful and positive individual experiences, just as I will be doing here. Yet the central contention remains: the argument from fruits is merely an observational note; it tells us nothing about the inward nature of religious experience, nothing about its psychological quality and meaning. Even when we stress, correctly, the broad social and cultural fruits of such experience, its adaptational significance and power in an evolutionary context, as Roy A. Rappaport (1999) does in his recent, influential volume (deeply indebted to James), *Ritual and Religion in the Making of Humanity*, we still fail to explain fully the underlying emotional and psychological nature of religious belief, the aspect of religion that drives particular, individual humans to embrace it with passion.

Finally, I am troubled by the empirical (or pragmatic) criterion because it raises these gigantic questions: Are the benefits we derive from religious experience genuine, lasting ones or do they mask deeper developmental, characterological problems which may never be addressed because of the turn to religion? Do people sometimes miraculously "find God," or undergo "spiritual change," or find their prayers for transformation answered because they wish to fly from their interpersonal and intrapsychic dilemmas, their developmental crises which stem from the actual, familial experiences they have undergone and never directly confronted, let alone resolved? At what price, in terms of an individual's psychological growth and maturity, does religion "work" as an alleviator of anxiety and conflict? To what extent are religious solutions magical solutions, backward as opposed to forward steps in the supremely important matter of growing up and becoming the person one was meant to be? Also, does the empiricist criterion work, or justify a "spiritual resolution," in every case in which we find it? Does anything go? Is my belief in spirits automatically justified and accepted by my peers because I, personally, discover it to be helpful, whatever that means? Is there nothing and no one in sight through which or through whom we may judge these matters, excluding the religionists themselves? Does our inquiry into religious experience collapse into mere relativism, losing all analytical, psychological, philosophic rigor? Does it suggest that whatever it is, if it works in relation to someone, somewhere, it is to be legitimated as "religious experience?" That seems terrible to me. Yet if we draw a line, if we reason and analyze and judge, the empiricist game is over; it instantly disappears, and that is because the "empiricist criterion" has nothing, absolutely nothing, in the way of a discursive position to support it. It is there only if we don't think. It dissolves of necessity the instant we begin to think, unless of course our thought is, Don't think!

To express the whole business somewhat differently, the empiricist criterion, for me, marks the beginning of religious inquiry, not the end. Although it looks spiffy enough, although it appears to be smartly accoutered with ideas, the empiricist criterion is on closer inspection intellectually drab, or threadbare. It leaves all the Hows and Whys entirely unanswered. But enough of provocative queries and generalities. Let's begin to explore—and I mean analytically—the specific topics with which this book will deal.

FAITH AND PRAYER

There is no tighter connection in the realm of religious experience than the connection between faith and prayer. They are spiritual symbionts, inextricably intertwined, breathing the same supersensible air, and destined to flourish, or to perish, together. Granting them each a single clause by way of compact definition, I would suggest the following: faith is the willful assertion that God not only exists but is there for one, available to one, involved caringly in one's life and affairs; prayer is faith in action, faith manifested, expressed, the actual calling upon God in the supernatural world. The mutuality, or perhaps the "system," is ironclad: if one has faith, one prays; if one prays, one demonstrates faith; if one fails to pray, faith slumbers; if one ceases to pray permanently, faith dies. And it goes without saying, of course, that faith's demise is also religion's demise. The religious literature supports all this completely; there just isn't any disagreement, anywhere. We have already noted James's remark that prayer "is the very soul and essence of religion" ([1902] 1987, 417). Here is a lengthy paragraph from Friedrich Heiler's classic study, *Prayer* ([1932] 1997, xiii), which presents comprehensively the orthodox position and which may be considered axiomatic. As far as this particular topic is concerned, the reader will require nothing further:

> Religious people, students of religion, theologians of all creeds and tendencies, agree in thinking that prayer is the central phenomenon of religion, the very hearthstone of all piety. Faith is, in Luther's judgment, "prayer and nothing but prayer. He who does not pray or call upon God in his hour of need, assuredly does not think of Him as God, nor does he give Him the honor that is His due." The great evangelistical mystic, Johann Arndt, constantly emphasized the truth that: "without prayer we cannot find God; prayer is the means by which we seek and find Him." Schleiermacher, the restorer of evangelical theology in the nineteenth century, observes in one of his sermons: "to be religious and to pray—that is really the same thing." Novalis, the poet of romanticism, remarks: "Praying is to religion what thinking is to philosophy." The same thought is expressed by the gifted evangelical divine, Richard Rothe, when he says, "the reli-

gious impulse is essentially the impulse to pray. It is by prayer, in fact, that the process of the individual religious life is governed, the process of the gradual fulfillment of God's indwelling in the individual and his religious life. Therefore, the non-praying man is rightly considered to be religiously dead."

For the naturalistic, psychological analysis to come, this is the upshot: to get at the essence of prayer is to get at the essence of faith; to get at the essence of faith is to get at the essence of religion. Of course we will look at the issue of faith's nature directly, in its own right, but we must always bear in mind as we go that our developing explanation of prayer is a developing explanation of faith and hence of religious experience. To turn the coin over, a full-fledged naturalistic understanding of religion requires little more than a full-fledged naturalistic understanding of prayer.

Faith, declares James (following Tolstoy), is more than a mere doctrinal or intellectual assertion about the existence of God; indeed, it is "among the forces *by which men live*" ([1902] 1987, 452). It is "a biological as well as a psychological condition," an actual "state," or "faith-state" as James puts it (452), which contributes immeasurably to an individual's overall well-being, to his joy and inner contentment, his psychological security, his biological integrity. Moreover, when faith is critically shaken, when the faith-state for whatever reason disappears, the individual finds himself in crisis, in "collapse" (452), wounded organismically in a life-threatening way. One of James's subjects declares that the imagined absence of his "communion" with God "would be chaos. I cannot conceive of life without its presence" (70). Declares another, "God is more real to me than any thought or thing or person. I feel his presence, . . . his love for me, and care for my safety. . . . Without it life would be a blank, a desert, a shoreless, trackless waste" (70–71). Similar notes are struck in Oxtoby's "The Islamic Tradition" (1996, 375), where the Arabic word for faith, namely *iman*, turns out to be synonymous with Islam itself and defined as "total surrender of the human will and destiny to the will of God." Oxtoby describes such "surrender" as "an inner personal commitment" which affords the individual—precisely as in James—"a personal sense of safety and well-being in God's providential care" (375). Calvin (ca. 1550) too supports faith's elemental nature, tying it directly to what he calls a "sense of divinity." Calvin writes, "there is within the human mind, and that by natural instinct, a sense of divinity. This we take to be beyond controversy. . . . God frequently renews and sometimes increases this awareness. . . . There is no nation so barbarous, no people so savage, that they do not have a pervasive belief in God. . . . There has been no region since the beginning of the world, no city, no home, that could exist without religion; this fact in itself points to a sense of divinity in-scribed in the hearts of all people" (1997, 57). As for recent declarations of this kind, we have Dr. Herbert Benson maintaining in his book *Timeless Healing: The Power and Biology of Belief* (1996) that we are "wired for God" (195). Belief in the Deity, says Benson, "is a primal motive or a survival in-stinct" (195). Humans are "genetically encoded with a need for and nour-ishment from faith. . . . When people call upon faith, they activate neurologic pathways for self-healing" (jacket). James's faith-state, then, has been accorded an explicitly genetical status.

We come now to a watershed: the discussion to follow is largely devoted to deconstructing the faith-state, or *iman*, or the sense of divinity, or Benson's idea that we are "wired for God," through a psychological expla-nation of prayer. It is devoted to such a deconstruction because this author is unable to accept the biological, genetic, elemental propositions which underpin the notion of the faith-state as a whole. By the time this state ap-pears, even inchoately, by the time it is expressed and actualized through prayer and the belief in supernaturals, it is already a packed and layered complexity, a subjective, emotional, composite, with years of growth and development behind it. Indeed, not only has the entire preverbal and hugely formative stage of our existence transpired, but the early, crucial pe-riod of verbal communication (communion) has also left its considerable mark upon the human creature (nurture as opposed to nature). In a word, we don't "get religion" at the start, or anywhere near the start. We have been living and interacting intensely with other people for a considerable duration before we sense the Divine. And when we do get religion, when we do begin to experience the faith-state, it inherits and addresses the prob-lems and the tendencies that were there before it was there, the problems and the tendencies that derive from the aforesaid intense interactions.

To come upon the human scene and to call faith elemental is like coming to the play shortly after intermission and attempting to interpret the subse-quent scenes without the benefit of the opening act, or acts. No matter how astute and clever the tardy theatergoer, he will not be in a position to under-stand fully what is occurring right before his eyes. Note, for example, the following questions which arise like mountains precisely because the roots of the faith-state are ignored in the materials we've just cited. Why is the faith-state so important for some—a matter of life and death, in fact—and not so important for others? Why do certain people collapse when faith re-cedes while others are just fine? How is it that for many the faith-state is of no significance at all? What are the developmental, psychological factors at work during both the preverbal and early verbal phases (as well as later childhood and adolescence), which contribute to this disparate human situation, this disparate human behavior? Granted, it may make some sort of sense to suggest that we are "wired" for language, or aggression, or sexuality, but faith in a deity? Wired for that? What about all the nonbelievers on the planet? There are millions of them. Are they genetic sports, the result of faulty wiring? Is there not a faint inquisitional smell lurking around this position? Surely it is preferable theoretically to say we are wired for something more basic, more elemental than faith, of which faith, and religion, are relatively mature, symbolic expressions—I mean in a temporal sense: wired for attachment perhaps; or for holding on intrapsychically to security-inducing, awe-inspiring parental presences. If we take this line, we can apprehend perfectly well why masses of people turn away from God only to make gods out of other things: money, or the state, or a lover.

We have noted the inextricable tie between faith and prayer. Does this tie suggest, by way of Benson's genetic reasoning, that we are wired for prayer? If millions do not believe, do not live in a faith-state, then assuredly millions more do not pray. What are we to say of them? Are they genetical miscarriages too? I don't think so. But I do suspect that (just as with faith) we may be wired for what prayer does, namely attach us to powerful, projective, parental presences (Christ, Allah, Brahma, Yahweh), allow us to communicate with someone or something that offers us, in our wishful imaginations, many of the items we crave elementally: emotional security, narcissistic pampering, a sense of empowerment, the inward conviction that we are lovable and good. Clearly then, what James and Benson and the others regard as elemental or given, namely the faith-state, the tie to God, the comforting reliance on the Deity, the intimate, prayerful communion with supernatural beings—all this we must subject to psychological exploration so that we may grasp in analytic terms both where it comes from and what it means. The bedrock of religion, namely faith, is not our bedrock but our digging place, our archaeological site, as it were, where we delve for clues to the origins of things. As I stated earlier, I appreciate how annoying such activity must be for the believer: all that psychological probing and peering into sacred ground. Yet there may be a compensatory benefit, or in James's terms another kind of fruit, awaiting the analytical operation. I refer to an enhanced understanding of ourselves and our fellow creatures; to a deepened insight into our human needs and fears, our basic nature as it arises in homely fashion through our interactions with others; to a less projective and hence more honest relationship with the world around us. Such enlightenment (in a double sense that includes the historical meaning) springs from our wonderful tendency as humans to work at perceiving the world as fully, as directly, as we can, our wonderful tendency to work at seeing, comprehending, digesting the essence of things, no matter what it suggests about our place in the universe and our final destiny as mortals. Surely this program of enlightenment has its own fruits, its own spirit, its own emotional and mental rewards.

THEORETICAL BACKDROP: FREUD AND WINNICOTT

The modern psychology of religion is deeply embedded in the writings of Winnicott and Freud. It is time now to examine their famous discussions and, in the light of them, to indicate more fully our own theoretical bent. First Freud.

That supernatural entities, including the gods and spirits of the religious realm, are human fabrications with no basis in reality is an idea as old as the hills. It turns up in ancient India, China, Greece, and Rome, and it appears sporadically in various regions of the world throughout the course of history (Smart 1969, 499). However, it is only during the past five centuries, in the scientific societies of the west, that what we may term a "projection theory of religion" (Hinnells 1995, 392) achieves widespread influence, largely through the work of powerful thinkers such as Montaigne, Diderot, Hobbes, Hume, Feuerbach, Marx, and Nietzsche. "Religion is the dream of the human mind," writes Feuerbach (1989, xix) in 1841 echoing the skeptical conclusions of the Enlightenment. "God is dead" pronounces Nietzsche (1974, 125) in 1882 expressing succinctly the doubt and disbelief that have flourished on the Continent for more than three-hundred years. In this way, when Freud in 1927 pens what we may regard as a cornerstone of the modern psychology of religion, namely *The Future of an Illusion* (Freud [1927] 1964), he is working within a well-established tradition, especially in the German-speaking world. While there are no direct references to Feuerbach in Freud's corpus, we can hardly doubt that Freud knew Feuerbach's notorious book, with its depictions of religion as a "dream" and theology as an "illusion" (Feuerbach 1989, xviii–xix). As for the profundity of Nietzsche's influence on Freud—there really is no other way to express the matter—it is by now an uncontested fact. What is fresh and vital about Freud's projection theory is Freud's approach to the origin and nature of projection. The religious world does not arise from projection in some diffuse, general sense; it arises, in significant measure, from projection as it is rooted in the individual's early, foundational experience, the years during which parental ministrations protect the neonate and the child from both the dangers of the external world and from the anxieties that perforce attend the condition of helplessness, of absolute dependency. At their foundation, religious projections are unconscious.

"Religious ideas," writes Freud ([1927]1964, 47), "are illusions, fulfillments of the oldest, strongest and most urgent wishes of mankind." He goes on:

> The secret of their strength lies in the strength of these wishes. As we already know, the terrifying impression of helplessness in childhood aroused the need for protection—for protection through love—which was provided by the father; and the recognition that this helplessness lasts throughout life made it necessary to cling to the existence of a father, but this time a more powerful one. Thus the benevolent rule of a divine Providence allays our fear of the dangers of life; the establishment of a moral world-order ensures the fulfillment of the demands of justice, which have so often remained unfulfilled in human civilization; and the prolongation of earthly existence in a future life provides the local and temporal framework in which these wish-fulfillments shall take place. (47–48)

In this way, when individuals confront the "crushingly superior forces of nature" (30), as well as the shortcomings of society and the tragedies of personal loss, they fall back upon an "infantile model" (31) and tenaciously cling to the notion that "over each one of us there watches a benevolent Providence which is only seemingly stern and which will not suffer us to become a plaything of the over-mighty and pitiless forces of nature" (26). Indeed, nature itself is "humanized" (22) through mankind's projective "longing" for the "father" and for "the gods" (24). It boils down, then, to our helplessness at life's inception, and to our helplessness throughout life's course:

> When the growing individual finds that he is destined to remain a child forever, that he can never do without protection against strange superior powers, he lends those powers the features belonging to the figure of the father; he creates for himself the gods whom he dreads, whom he seeks to propitiate, and whom he nevertheless entrusts with his own protection. Thus his longing for a father is a motive identical with his need for protection against the consequences of his human weakness. The defense against childish helplessness is what lends its characteristic features to the adult's reaction to the helplessness which *he* has to acknowledge—a reaction which is precisely the formation of religion. (35)

We might note here Freud's sensitivity to religion's adaptive, "emotional value" ([1927] 1964, 86), his recognition of the soothing, comforting role religion plays in the world—something Freud's critics generally ignore when they present his position. "Life is hard to bear," states Freud (21), and without "religious ideas" would "not be tolerable" for many individuals (28). Nor is Freud unaware of the mother's role in all this, although he gives the mother short shrift in his analysis as a whole: "The mother, who satisfies the child's hunger, becomes its first love-object and certainly also its first protection against all the undefined dangers which threaten it in the external world—its first protection against anxiety, we may say" (34). However, in spite of religion's consolatory powers and soothing, adaptational functions, it is, finally, regressive, infantile, irrational—the product of "ignorance and intellectual weakness" (70). Religion bears witness, Freud asserts, to humanity's fixation on "wishful illusions," to its present state of "blissful hallucinatory confusion," to its "disavowal of reality" (71).

In a famous, perhaps provocative figure, Freud maintains that religion is "the universal obsessional neurosis of humanity" (71). And what of the future? It is not without hope: "most . . . infantile neuroses are overcome spontaneously in the course of growing up," writes Freud, and "this is especially true of the obsessional neuroses" (70). Thus, "a turning-away from religion" is "bound to occur" sooner or later "with the fatal inevitability of a process of growth" (71). As a matter of fact, "we [now] find ourselves . . . in the middle of that phase of development" (71). God may not be dead, as Nietzsche maintained, but he is surely dying, according to Freud. "Men cannot remain children forever" (81). The "neurotic relics" which ultimately comprise "religious teachings" are destined to be abandoned (72); "infantilism" is "destined to be surmounted" (81), no matter how passionately individuals and groups strive to preserve it. Freud calls this, "education to reality" (81), or the renunciation of all illusions. "The voice of the intellect is a soft one," Freud concludes, "but it does not rest till it has gained a hearing" (87). Freud had other interesting and controversial things to say about religious matters in such books as *Civilization and Its Discontents* and *Moses and Monotheism*, but it is *The Future of an Illusion* which has left an indelible mark on the modern psychology of religion.

Working for many years with children and adults at the Paddington Green Children's Hospital in London, Winnicott reached conclusions very different than Freud's in regard to the religious "illusions" of humankind. Where Freud sees obsessional neurosis and infantilism, Winnicott sees normative, healthy adaptation and creativity, an inventive and vital tendency on the part of people to achieve lifelong security and inner well-being as they cope with separation and crisis in what he calls "the intermediate area" (Winnicott 1971, xi), a psychological zone somewhere between the poles of objectivity and subjectivity. He writes, "of every individual who

has reached to the stage of being a unit with a limiting membrane and an
outside and an inside, it can be said that there is an inner reality to that individual, an inner world that can be rich or poor and can be at peace or in a
state of war" (1971, 2). Winnicott continues:

> my claim is that if there is a need for this double statement there is also
> a need for a triple one: the third part of the life of a human being, a part
> that we cannot ignore, is an intermediate area of experiencing, to
> which inner reality and external life both contribute. It is an area that
> is not challenged, because no claim can be made on its behalf except
> that it shall exist as a resting-place for the individual engaged in the
> perpetual human task of keeping inner and outer reality separate yet
> interrelated. . . . I am therefore studying the substance of *illusion*, that
> which is allowed to the infant, and which in adult life is inherent in art
> and religion, and yet becomes the hallmark of madness when an adult
> puts too powerful a claim on the credulity of others, forcing them to
> acknowledge a sharing of illusion that is not their own. We can share a
> respect for *illusory experience*, and if we wish we may collect together
> and form a group on the basis of the similarity of our illusory experi-
> ences. This is a natural root of grouping among human beings. (1971,
> 2–3)

Let's turn now, briefly, to Winnicott's depictions of the manner in which the
"intermediate area," or the province of "illusion," develops in the life of the
individual.

Our development from the early period of helplessness to the attainment of separation and autonomy has a magical and in some sense paradoxical aspect to it. It is bound up integrally with mothering, with
substitute objects, and with that "intermediate area" in which substitution
finds its full, phenomenological expression, namely play. In the words of
Winnicott (1971, 12–14), the "good-enough mother" begins by adapting almost completely to the "infant's needs." As time goes on, "she adapts less
and less completely . . . according to the infant's growing ability to deal with
her failure" through his own experience. If all goes well, the infant can actually "gain" from his "frustration" by developing his own idiosyncratic
style of relative independence. What is essential is that the mother give the
baby, through her good-enough care, the illusion that "there is an external
reality that corresponds to the infant's own capacity to create." It is precisely within this area of creativity that the infant will begin to make his
transition away from the maternal figure by finding, or discovering, "transitional objects"—blankets, teddy bears, storybooks—which afford him

the magical or illusory belief that he is moving toward, or staying with, the caretaker at the same time that he is moving away from her or giving her up. Because the transitional object is discovered in the real world it has a kind of objectivity, or facticity; because the child projects into it his own idiosyncratic wishes and needs, it also takes on a subjective cast. It is both found and created. Such magic, such illusion, such creativity provides the child with his primary link to the cultural realm, to the religious and artistic symbols that comprise the shared, illusory reality of grown-ups. "The matter of illusion," declares Winnicott (1971, 13), "is one that belongs inherently to human beings and that no individual finally solves for himself or herself." The "task of reality-acceptance is never completed. . . . No human being is free from the strain of relating inner and outer reality" (13). It is the "intermediate area of experience" including art and religion that provides "relief from the strain" and that is "in direct continuity with the play area of the small child who is lost in play" (13). In this way, "there is a direct development from transitional phenomena to playing, and from playing to shared playing, and from this to cultural experiences" (1971, 51).

In order to "get the idea of playing," Winnicott goes on (1971, 51), it is "helpful to think of the preoccupation that characterizes the playing of the young child. The content does not matter. What matters is the near-withdrawal state, akin to the concentration of older children and adults" (51). Playing "involves the body," is "inherently exciting," and transpires amid the experience of a "non-purposive state" which is marked above all by "relaxation" (52). It is "only in playing," Winnicott concludes (52), that the "child or adult is free to be creative" and that the world he inhabits becomes "invested with a first-time-ever quality." Thus the good-enough mother permits the growing child to participate playfully in the first objects of his cultural experience and hence to find a method of separating from the parental figure while, paradoxically, maintaining the connection to that figure all in the same psychological moment.

I want to enrich these seminal notions with a citation or two from other psychoanalytic authors. Of the transitional object itself Greenacre (1971, 384) writes, "it represents not only the mother's breast and body but the total maternal environment as it is experienced in combination with sensations from the infant's body. It serves as a support and convoy during that period of rapid growth which necessitates increasing separation from the mother." We should also note that during this period "speech is in the process of formation" (384). Indeed, the creation and exploitation of the transitional realm derives from the same psychological impetus that lies behind the creation of the symbolical universe in general and the religious universe in particular. The driving need is to internalize the environment, to grip the external world and thus to answer the problem of loss with the kind of psychological mastery or control which Roheim (1955, 109) terms "dual-unity," the state of having the object at the symbolic level and of relinquishing the object at the level of reality.

To express the matter from another, related angle, because the infant's attachment is there before the other is experienced as other, the growing awareness of the caretaker as a "differentiated being" is itself "experienced as a loss" (Pine 1979, 226). True, there is an "objective" gain in "cognitive comprehension" as this process transpires. At the same time, however, there is the awareness that "certain treasured sensations are not part of the self but can come and go" (Pine 1979, 226). Accordingly, the presence of the early powerful attachment both facilitates and complicates our movement away from the mother, our growth as separate, differentiated creatures. It facilitates by providing us with a stable, loving internalization, a good object that endures and that leads us toward positive attachment to other people and toward the objects of culture (art and religion). It complicates because the experience of loss "permanently endows the relationship to the mother with painful undercurrents and sets up a developmental pathway that can be traversed in both directions," that is, toward progression and selfhood, or toward regression, hostility, and pathogenic absorption in the objects of the past (Pine 1979, 226). Here is the "dichotomous human condition" (Neubauer 1985, 139), the "forward maturational pulls" and the "neurotic backward attractions" (139) that all of us experience to one degree or another at various times in our lives. If we strive to exist "authentically," to look bravely and honestly at the truth of our relations with others and with ourselves, we have a reasonably good chance, as Rona Bank (1999, 131) expresses it in a recent paper on Winnicott, to know how it feels to be "humanly alive."

From Freud I will take the accurate, discriminating, related observations that (1) religious ideas comprise the fulfillment of humankind's most fervent wishes, and that (2) the strength of religious ideas, their persistent, tenacious hold upon the mind, is grounded in the strength of those wishes. What follows, especially in chapter 3, will work to reveal in meticulous fashion, through the aforementioned fine-grained analysis of prayer, precisely what those wishes are, their innermost quality, their underlying nature, their dynamic, magical essence. In doing this, I will set aside Freud's view of religion as "the universal obsessional neurosis of humanity," or the pan-human psychological malaise. There may be some sense in which this is so, and obviously during certain historical periods and in some individual instances religion does appear to be a self-persecuting, anxiety-laden sickness, at least in Western culture. Yet the overall picture, especially today, fails to support this view. When Freud describes religion as a "blissful hallucinatory confusion" he comes much nearer the mark, particularly in reference to prayer, as we'll eventually discover. No question the religious realm is obsessional, persistently urging participation upon its practitioners who frequently cannot survive apart from it, as we saw in James. But then, eating and sleeping and making love and just plain enjoying oneself are also in a loose, informal sense obsessional. When it comes to religion, I believe Freud's word is more aptly used in this soft, metaphorical manner.

Nor will I offer the father here as the primary figure in the realm of religious illusions; on the contrary, I find the maternal figure, or the maternal "object" to employ the terminology of object-relations theory, residing at the foundation, in the relational core from which the symbols of religion arise and flourish. By the time the father emerges as Deity in consciousness and ritual, He harbors within the complexity of His image the structuring, formative pre-Oedipal years during the course of which the young person's primary internalizations develop. The projective Father–God inherits the longings, the conflicts, the anxieties, the joys and exaltations—in a word, the goodness and the badness—of life's initial stages. Accordingly, the maternal object resides in the figure of the paternal Almighty and is always perceived there unconsciously by the worshipper. To put it somewhat differently, when development leads normally toward separation from the primary caregiver and the establishment of ego boundaries for the child, the father and his projection into the Father–God are there to catch and to hold the growing individual. Indeed, unless development leads away from the mother, particularly for young males (see Gilligan 1982), we are apt to get deep and lasting disturbance, distorted perception, inner turmoil, actual or emotional incest. Such disturbance within the spiritual realm is often acted out in occultism or wizardry or shamanism where the self-absorbed, all-powerful magician reflects the omnipotence and primary narcissism characteristic of the first relationship (see La Barre 1970).

To grow up and become persons we must reach the Oedipal level; we must find our way to the Father–God. However—and this is the point—we do not leave the maternal object behind when we do so. The whole of infantile life, the whole of early childhood, is absorbed into our religious wishing, at the center of which is the urge to join with the Almighty and hence to recapture (among other things) the sensation of inviolable security, or symbiosis. Thus, when we pray, we pray "from" the infant, "from" the child, as well as "from" the adolescent and adult. When we sense the presence of God, we sense Him "from" the infant and the child within, as well as "from" the wishes and the needs of the adult. This means of course that we behave religiously "from" the stage in which infant and child interact primarily with the maternal figure. It means that our religious life reaches all the way down to the infant and the child of the human inner world. When Freud ([1930] 1961, 20) turns to the religious realm in *Civilization and Its Discontents* and writes that "religious needs" are ultimately derived from the "infant's helplessness" and from the "longing for the father" aroused by such helplessness; and when he declares further that this causal scheme appears "incontrovertible" because he "cannot think of any need in childhood as strong as the need for a father's protection," he obliges us to ask, where is the mother in all of this, and where are those feelings tied to the child's interaction with the mother? Is not the need for symbiosis, union, or a close, protective relationship with the mothering figure as strong as the need for a father's protection, and is not the problem of separation from the parents, and especially from the mother, one of, if not the, key problems of childhood? It is almost astonishing that Freud could so neglect this aspect of human development in his analysis of the origin of religious needs, and, ultimately, of the cultural configurations which arise therefrom. Feminist literature usually calls this Freud's patriarchal bias, or Freud's patriarchal distortion of our psychological development. There will be no such bias, no such distortion here.

Turning to Winnicott, where the emphasis is upon the psychic inner world as it takes shape in and through the relationship with the good-enough mother, we begin to grasp in earnest the emotive-perceptual origin of the supernatural realm—how and why it discovers its wishful magical way into the life of the individual and the group. As I suggested very briefly in my earlier summary, we readily adopt the supernatural when we come upon it in our "cultural space" because we've been accustomed to residing within something very like it from the inception of our internalizing awareness, our egotic existence as differentiated, bounded entities. We've been there all along. For several years (ages 2–6) we've been creating a personal, subjective universe of illusory objects (dolls, teddies, storybooks, blankets) from our surrounding reality and on the inside where the internalized presence of the parental object completes the illusory scheme and thus serves as our inward companion, our inward guardian and guide, the intrapsychic version of the proverbial "god of the nursery." Perceptually, we've taken the caregiver inside and set her/him up as the emotional scaffold on which we will build our emerging, differentiated characters. In this way, we are used to living inwardly with powerful, unseen, "supernatural" presences; we are used to communing affectively, even verbally (as we seek out patterns of attachment) with loving, invisible internalizations which we've fashioned out of our real familial interactions with the actual people who surround us during the course of our early growth. When culture offers us a supernatural parent or companion (God), a "big one" who can't be seen but who nevertheless exists and cares, we understand immediately. Indeed, we're experts in such matters of perception and emotion because they correspond to what we've been doing for ourselves in the transitional realm of illusion, or the intermediate area, since we confronted the ominous yet enticing need for separation from the caretaker, differentiation from the caretaker, in our own experience.

We're eager to join in with the projective play of the social realm because, like everyone else, we too are hungry for attachment and support, for convoy, as we begin to "go it alone." We never lose this hunger, or this method of allaying it, although some of us may lose our traditional religion. Furthermore, when the culture actually shows us symbols of the supernatural, Bibles, pictures, statues, churches, in other words, "proofs" of the supernatural's reality, "proofs" that empirically legitimate spiritual belief and conduct, we are as little ones even more perceptually impelled toward subscription. Here is the Divine in actuality. Just as we have transitional objects and the actual parent to support our internalizations and subsequent projections in the intermediate area, so we have symbolical versions of the Deity, His tracks and His traces, to support His existence in the cultural sphere, our emerging new home. In one sentence, the development of religious faith comprises an emotional, perceptual continuity from the early period of human existence to the advent of the cultural order several years later.

Remember, the human infant is not simply weak and needy at the start; he is dependent on the caregiver for his very survival. Accordingly, the bond of attachment between baby and mother becomes as powerful as any in nature. Yet to survive and to flourish as a person the little one must discover an avenue away from the caregiver and toward the cultural world beyond, the world in which he will one day have his life and being. The signal task of early childhood (as we'll see in detail in chapter 2) is a transitional task, which means a transition away from the primary object toward other people and things, which serve to replace the receding, care-giving unit. We don't simply give up the parent; we give the parent up as we create, as we play, as we substitute. And our substitutions are vital in decreasing our anxiety to the point where we can do the giving up and move on developmentally. When the child discovers his transitional objects, when he both finds and fashions his substitutes for the maternal figure, he is in the same adaptive, anxiety-reducing perceptual mode that he is in when, later, he turns to the spiritual realm to address his ongoing wishes and needs. He discovers the supernatural caregiver who begins to replace the natural one, and he also creates the supernatural caregiver out of his own unconscious proclivities as they intermesh with cultural presentations. For this is how we've set it up as humans: to go forward and backward at the same time, to stay with the object through the realm of surrogates and to move away from the object through the realm of surrogates. We play it both ways, because we want to, and because, in the realm of illusion, we perceptually can.

ANTECEDENTS OF THE FAITH-STATE AND ULTIMATE POLARITIES

What James calls the faith-state is simply the continuation of this illusory perceptual behavior into adulthood. One proceeds to believe in the supernatural caretaker, who gradually merges intrapsychically with the internalized object of the early years. The Deity grows out of the object. For the majority, such growth transpires without complication through the combined powers of unconscious longing, unconscious anxiety, and societal urging, even as reason or empiric perception takes up its place within the mind. Indeed, reason may well come to support the illusory sphere through compelling theological argument. The world must have had a beginning. Who but God could have fashioned such an overwhelming externality? Erik Erikson (1964, 153) expresses it this way:

> What begins as hope in the individual infant is in its mature form faith, a sense of superior certainty not essentially dependent on evidence or reason. . . . [Religion] has shrewdly played into man's most child-like needs, not only by offering eternal guarantees for an omniscient power's benevolence (if properly appeased) but also by magic words and significant gestures, soothing sounds and soporific smells—an infant's world. . . . Yet at the height of its historical function [religion] has played another, corresponding role, namely that of giving concerted expression to adult man's need to provide the young and the weak with a world-image sustaining hope. Here it must not be forgotten that religious world-images have at least contained some recognition (and this is more than radical rationalism could claim until the advent of psychoanalysis) of the abysmal alienations—from the self and from others—which are the human lot. For along with a fund of hope, an inescapable alienation is also bequeathed to life by the first stage, namely, a sense of threatening separation from the matrix, a possible loss of hope, and the uncertainty whether the "face darkly" will brighten again with recognition and charity.

Thus faith, as I suggested earlier, is merely the willful, wishful, hopeful choice to believe, that's all. The faith-state is living in that choice. "Faith is the belief that God is real," states Max Lucado (1999, 121); "it isn't complicated, or mysterious, or mystical. It is the choice to believe that God is always available, just waiting for your touch." Accordingly, the lack of faith, or "unbelief," writes Ole Hallesby ([1948] 1979, 25), is an "attribute of the will," a "refusal to see," a refusal to "go to Jesus." As for prayer's role in the matter, I suggested that earlier too. Prayer is simply the clearest and most dramatic manifestation of one's belief, one's faith-state, for after all, if one is talking aloud, or speaking inwardly, to an unseen, supernatural entity, if one is not only going about in the belief that He is there, but communing with Him on a weekly, or daily, or even hourly basis in many instances, there can hardly be a dispute about the presence of one's "faith," the integrity of one's "faith-state," the actuality of one's choice to believe. What begins as hopeful transitional behavior in the intermediate area of childhood metamorphoses into hopeful transitional behavior in the intermediate area of adulthood. In both cases, creative, playful illusion, designed to allay anxiety and to increase potentiality by uniting the practitioner with a version of the all-powerful object, is the order of the day. Two further considerations come to mind here, and with them I will conclude this introduction.

First, James's notion that spiritual doctrine, spiritual belief, and the faith-state which arises therefrom are without naturalistic, material antecedents is simply mistaken. James writes, "the whole force of the Christian religion, . . . so far as belief in the divine personages determines the prevalent attitude of the believer, is in general exerted by the instrumentality of pure ideas, of which nothing in the individual's past experience directly serves as a model" (James [1902] 1987, 55). But there is something in the "individual's past experience" which "directly serves as a model." The early period and in particular the relation of the infant and child to the caregiver "directly serves as a model." Indeed, as we have seen and will continue to see, it is the internalizing, creative behaviors of the little one in the intermediate area that lead directly from the realm of transitional play to the illusory realm of religious faith, with its supernatural entities (gods, angels) and its spiritual practices (prayer, sacrifice). James was, needless to say, supremely aware of the role of the subconscious in the forging of religious life. He maintains in another place ([1902] 1987, 74),

> our impulsive belief is . . . always what set up the original body of truth, and our philosophy is but its showy verbalized translation. The immediate assurance is the deep thing in us, the argument is but a surface exhibition. Instinct leads, intelligence does but follow. If a per-

son feels the presence of a living God after the fashion shown by my quotations, your critical arguments, be they never so superior, will vainly set themselves to change his faith. Please observe, however, that I do not yet say that it is *better* that the subconscious and non-rational should thus hold primacy in the religious realm. I confine myself to simply pointing out that they do so hold it as a matter of fact.

What James could not uncover about the specific contents of the causal subconscious in 1902, we can uncover a hundred years later through our newly won psychological insight: It is the longing, the anxiety, the magical empowerment of human infancy and childhood that subconsciously implodes into cultural space and catalyzes the emergence of the religious realm as it is creatively fashioned by symbol-making grownups capable of conceiving gods, the illusions of spiritual adulthood. What for James was best explained by recourse to the supernatural ([1902] 1987, 467) is explained with perfect clarity today through reliance on the natural sphere alone, through reliance on real people interacting with one another in real families and real societies in the real world, and nowhere else. When James writes ([1902] 1987, 106) in an Emersonian moment that the "spirit of the universe" is "your own subconscious self," we respectfully reply that "your own subconscious self" is the trace of the human relations you have known (and internalized) in your interpersonal past, along with, of course, the genetic endowment with which the universe has blessed or cursed you willy nilly.

Second, the issues that emerge from the pursuit of a "projection theory of religion" (Hinnells 1995, 392) engage two of our most rooted, powerful tendencies as people. On the one hand, we crave relation with, attachment to, the world, not merely as it touches us immediately as microcosms, but as it holds us, contains us, at the macrocosmic level of experience. We want to believe in a world that has meaning, that cares, that is benign and hopeful because we can't help seeing the world projectively as an extension of ourselves and of the big ones from whom our selves issued forth psychologically in the beginning. Also, and profoundly, we do not wish to confront the separation, the terror, the naughtment that lurks in death. We do not wish to be snatched from our projective psychic containers and consigned forever to egotic and hence to cosmic nothingness. We want to live as securely, as free of ontological stress, as we possibly can.

On the other hand, we don't want illusions, we don't want self-deceptions, we don't want to be cut off from the realities of our condition, our situation in the world. We want to see, to perceive clearly, honestly, bravely with our evolutionally big brains and our reason, no matter what the price we pay in emotional insecurity and death fear. The power of religious issues, the passion in religious questions, springs largely from this radical and possibly evolutional antithesis, both sides of which harbor basic aspects of our nature as a species of life. As I stated near this chapter's inception, my purpose here is to offer a naturalistic alternative to the supernaturalism we find in James, and in a thousand other writings which in one way or another reflect James's perspective. Perhaps at this juncture we comprehend more fully than we did toward the outset why ponderable alternatives as opposed to ironclad refutations are all that we can expect, or hope for, in this area. If, as James maintains, belief is natural and self-enhancing for the believer, then so is nonbelief for the one who turns away through keen, considered judgment. If projection is what we do and have always done as people, then withdrawing our projections is what we also do, and increasingly do, as psychological analysis helps us to grasp our unconscious motives. Is there another aspect of our fundamental humanity that goes off like this in two opposing yet perfectly natural directions?

REFERENCES

Bank, R. 1999. "Mythic Perspectives and Perspectives on Truth: Approaching Winnicott." *Psychoanalytic Review* 86: 109–36.

Benson, H. 1996. *Timeless Healing: The Power and Biology of Belief*. New York: Scribner's.

Calvin, J. 1997. "On the Natural Knowledge of God." In *The Christian Theology Reader*, ed. A. McGrath. London: Blackwell, 57.

Erikson, E. 1964. *Insight and Responsibility*. New York: Norton.

Feuerbach, L. [1841] 1989. *The Essence of Christianity*. Trans. G. Eliot. Amherst, N.Y.: Prometheus Books.

Freud, S. [1927] 1964. *The Future of an Illusion*. Trans. J. Strachey. New York: Doubleday.

Freud, S. [1930] 1961. *Civilization and Its Discontents*. Trans. J. Strachey. New York: Norton.

Gilligan, C. 1982. *In a Different Voice*. Cambridge: Harvard University Press.

Greenacre, P. 1971. "The Transitional Object and the Fetish." *Psychoanalytic Quarterly* 40: 384–85.

Hallesby, O. [1948] 1979. *Prayer*. Trans. C. Carlsen. Leicester, England: Intervarsity Press.

Heiler, F. [1932] 1997. *Prayer: A Study in the History and Psychology of Religion*. New York: Oxford University Press.

Hinnells, J., ed. 1995. *The Penguin Dictionary of Religions*. London: Penguin Books.

James, W. [1902] 1987. *The Varieties of Religious Experience*. New York: Library of America.

La Barre, W. 1970. *The Ghost Dance: Origins of Religion*. New York: Doubleday.

Lucado, M. 1999. *The Gift for All People*. Sisters, Oreg.: Multnomah Publishers.

Neubauer, P. 1985. "Preoedipal Objects and Object Primacy." *The Psychoanalytic Study of the Child* 40: 163–82.

Nietzsche, F. 1974. *The Gay Science*. New York: Vintage Books.

Oxtoby, W. 1996. "The Islamic Tradition." In *World Religions: Western Traditions*, ed. W. Oxtoby. New York: Oxford, 352–491.

Pine, F. 1979. "On the Pathology of the Separation-Individuation Process." *International Journal of Psychoanalysis* 60: 225–42.

Rappaport, R. 1999. *Ritual and Religion in the Making of Humanity*. New York: Cambridge University Press.

Roheim, G. 1955. *Magic and Schizophrenia*. Bloomington: Indiana University Press.

Smart, N. 1969. *The Religious Experience of Mankind*. New York: Scribner's.

Winnicott, D. 1971. *Playing and Reality*. New York: Basic Books.

CHAPTER 2

THE PSYCHOLOGICAL MATRIX OF PRAYER AND FAITH

PART ONE

Because the world of infancy and childhood is not an easy one to capture discursively, because as adults we run the risk of ascribing to the very young aims and motives at work in us rather than in them (see Kirschner 1996),[1] I would prefer to explore the religious realm psychologically without also exploring life's early period; but alas, there is just no hope of getting at the truth that way. Religious behavior is an outgrowth, a development, in a special sense an expression of this period with its symbiotic attachments, its blissful transformations, its powerful, persistent anxieties, attunements, frustrations, and fears. Indeed, if psychoanalytic psychology has made a lasting and valuable contribution to the understanding of religious conduct, it is in precisely this area. Focusing momentarily on the originator, we must point out that even Freud's opponents in the matter of spirituality, even those who ultimately disagree with his outlook, acknowledge the correctness of rooting the psychological study of religion in the ground where human existence commences. Although Freud's view of religion as a regression to "the earliest psychic strata" demands "rethinking," writes W. W. Meissner (1984, vii–viii), although it is loaded with Freud's "prejudices" and "inner conflicts," it nevertheless brings us by virtue of Freud's "genius" to the "interface of man's religious life with his psychological life in a more poignant and telling way than ever before in human history." In spite of several misemphases and outright errors, maintains Ana-Maria Rizzuto (1979, 28), Freud's view of "God" is "essentially correct" and comprises a "major contribution" to our "understanding of man," and in particular "of man's lifelong use of early imagos and object representations." Thus we really have no choice. Our business in what follows must be to indicate the "early imagos" and "object representations" that comprise the foundational "strata" of religious belief. An additional issue arises at this juncture.

As everyone knows, for the past thirty or forty years psychoanalysis as theory and therapy has been attacked by a variety of philosophical skeptics, from Adolf Grünbaum to Frederick Crews, from Richard Webster to Frank Cioffi. It has also been partially superseded by biological and pharmacological approaches (see Hale Jr., 1995). Why then does psychoanalysis continue to "live" and to live vigorously, as John Horgan (1996, 106) expresses it in *The Scientific American*? Horgan replies, "one explanation may be that [Freud's work], in spite of its flaws, still represents a compelling framework within which to ponder our mysterious selves." Another may be that "psychotherapists of all stripes still tend to share two of Freud's core beliefs: One is that our behavior, thoughts and emotions stem from unconscious fears and desires, often rooted in childhood experiences. The other is that with the help of a trained therapist, we can understand the source of our troubles and thereby obtain some relief." Yet there may be just a tad more to it than that, for as the aforementioned skeptic Richard Webster (1995, 8), whose major work is titled *Why Freud Was Wrong*, puts it, psychoanalysis "has every claim to be regarded as richer and more original than any other single intellectual tradition in the twentieth century."

While psychoanalysis may sometimes get it wrong in the "details," writes Daniel Liechty (echoing Ernest Becker), it still "claims a hold on us because it is so close to the truth we all experience. Even the least introspective among us knows that we are anxiety-ridden creatures whose conscious will is fooled and distorted by unconscious forces. If Freud was wrong on any or all of the details, he continues to fascinate because he looked at this condition and did not turn away into the pious platitudes of philosophy or religion. . . . His place will always be one of respect amongst those who also did not look away" (Liechty 1999, 7). In all of this, by the way, I am not suggesting that the philosophical skeptics, Grünbaum, Crews, Cioffi, and others, continue to hold sway in professional circles. On the contrary, their arguments against psychoanalysis have been effectively countered, even refuted, by a number of writers including most notably Donald Levy (1996, 172), whose landmark work, *Freud among the Philosophers*, deals in depth with the major attackers and concludes as follows:

Psychoanalysis is amply equipped to respond to the philosophical criticism that has been mounted against it thus far. No good philosophical arguments against it have been produced, and much empirical evidence supports it. It is no wonder that psychoanalysis has been experienced, from different viewpoints, as a radical shift in human thought, and that many have treated it as an advance in our self-understanding—precisely the extension or unfolding of individual subjectivity that it claims to be.

Mindful of the pitfalls, then, and with Levy's endorsement ringing in our ears, let us begin to indicate precisely the source from which will flow our analytical view of prayer and faith.

Psychoanalysis after Freud

The psychoanalytic direction from which I will be approaching the religious realm is ultimately indebted to Freud, but it is indebted directly and overwhelmingly to several of his followers whose work becomes prominent in the decades following Freud's death. Hence, I will not be relying here on the Oedipus complex, sexuality, the "discharge" of aggressive and libidinal "drives," the primary role of the father in emotional life, the wish-fulfillment theory of dreams, or the phylogenetic unconscious (Mr. Hyde of Jekyll and Hyde fame) as it is inherited from our primitive, Darwinian past. I will rely instead upon the work of (1) Melanie Klein, with its emphasis on the child's tendency to internalize the environment, to create a world of internalized objects, or presences, from which arise a number of early, primal fantasies as well as a number of early, primal defenses, most notably projective identification and splitting the residues of which are frequently found in the emotional and intellectual lives of adults; (2) the work of Ronald Fairbairn, with its powerful insistence (supported by vivid clinical case studies) that newcomers to this world do not seek primarily to release their "instinctual energies" but to find and connect with the caregiver, the object upon whom their physical and emotional well-being depends. Put simply, the baby seeks the breast as opposed to a "reduction of tension"; (3) the work of Donald Winnicott, with its seminal notions of good-enough mothering, the foundation of normal cognitive and emotional life; transitional objects (blankets, teddy bears, storybooks), those substitutive items to which the child turns as he copes with separation from the caregiver (disillusionment); potential space, the inner, psychological realm where the child learns to fashion a reality from the creative capacities of his own mind as they interact with the external environment. This primary, persistent illusion (the aftermath of disillusionment) comprises a synthesizing, epistemological complement to our traditional notions of subjective and objective. Reality, holds Winnicott, is always both inner and outer simultaneously, is always a mix; (4) the work of John Bowlby and his followers (René Spitz, Mary Ainsworth, Robert Karen), which underscores the decisive role of attachment and loss in our maturational growth. For Bowlby, soothing, secure attachment to an available caregiving figure is the *sine qua non* of satisfactory human development, and early separation (either actual, physical separation or the kind of separation that is fostered by an ambivalent or rejecting parent) is the root cause of human malaise. Bowlby's lifelong aim was to put psychoanalysis squarely on an empirical footing; (5) the work of Margaret Mahler and associates, where the issues of separation and attachment are explored in close connection with the child's biological and emotional need to differentiate himself/herself from the caretaker and gain a stable, separate identity. For Mahler, the struggle between separation and attachment, or differentiation and merger, is the elemental struggle of our being. Even as we manage to differentiate ourselves from the maternal presence we are devising, often unconsciously, a number of strategies for remerging with that presence at the mental-emotional level. The struggle between separation and union, says Mahler, ends only when we die; (6) the detailed, observational work of Daniel Stern, which concentrates upon the emotional and perceptual interactions of the early, dyadic relationship; the parent's attempt to attune herself to her child; the mutual delight of parent and child who act in synch with one another; the gradual creation of the newcomer's inner world where the caregiver's loving ministrations, internalized by the growing child, become the source of the inward companionship that most of us are able to experience when we are alone. The self as Stern conceives of it is based upon internalizations of the other; this gives us our wonderful capacity to sense the other's presence within even when the other is absent (in psychoanalytic circles this is called "dual-unity"); (7) the work of Christopher Bollas, where we come to appreciate the transformational role of the caregiver in the child's early years. Again and again the parent transforms the child's actual world, changing discomfort into pleasure, or relief: hunger into satiety, anxiety into security, wetness into dryness, and so forth. Bollas helps us to realize that a search for transformation in later life is often rooted unconsciously in a search for the original transformational object of childhood; (8) the work of Stephen Mitchell, with its emphasis upon the primary role of relations in human experience. For Mitchell, we are social to the root, and all our behaviors, whether in the spheres of work, play, family, worship, or intimacy, harbor some aspect of relationship, of human interaction, both at their primal, foundational source in the past and their more immediate, desire-driven source in the present. What each of these thinkers has in common with the rest is perhaps best expressed in Fairbairn's key notion, at the bedrock of present-day psychoanalysis, that the child seeks the object, the person, the relation, and not the discharge of his oral or anal instincts. Moving away from its early conceptualizations, from its close connection to the physical sciences of the nineteenth century, psychoanalysis has become a person-centered, relation-centered psychology, a psychology of object-relations, preoccupied primarily with the ways in which people interact with one another, and with the fantasies, or the projections, that invariably arise from those interactions.

I believe this overview underscores the extent to which modern psychoanalysis strives to approach human behavior from an empirical perspective, strives to avoid obtaining its data primarily from the ruminations of its theorists, strives in short to give clinical, observational studies a place of honor. Bowlby, Winnicott, Mahler, Stern: they look at children long and hard, and they fashion their analytic positions directly out of that looking. They do not come to children bearing axiomatic presuppositions (archetypes, for example) along with them. I am not suggesting that present-day psychoanalysts never employ inferential material as they go about their business, never take data from the analyses of adults and, in the light of that data, characterize the early interpersonal world of those very adults. Of course this occurs; indeed, it occurs of necessity. We can not climb into time-machines with our patients and travel backwards. We must in many instances interpret or read ourselves into the past, for if we let the past go we let the foundation go; we let the possible determinants of behavior go; we let one rich source of our insight go.

Yet increasingly in modern psychoanalysis inferential interpretation is influenced, even governed by, conclusions drawn from ongoing clinical research; increasingly the theorizers are the clinicians and the clinicians the theorizers. We will never, obviously, have perfect objectivity here, if there is such a thing. To study human beings, or better, to have certain human beings studying other human beings, will never lead to the kind of certitude that arises when certain human beings study, say, table salt. But we can try. In a cautious, responsible, healthily skeptical frame of mind we can try to be as objective as possible, try to discern what is there, actually there, try to make our analytical narratives jibe with what we believe to be the givens of human interaction during life's early stages, and later stages too, bearing in mind always that culture and hence experience are ceaselessly changing, even as we probe them. After all, what choice have we? Should we stop exploring the early period because we can't be perfectly objective about it?

Should we return to the Middle Ages, when the study of infants and children was nonexistent? Should we do for little monkeys and little rats what we won't do for ourselves? Or should we do the best we can and in a flexible, dialectical spirit bring our insight to our fellow creatures (both sick and well) who doubtless wish to enjoy all the knowledge they can gain, of both themselves and others? In my view, there is only one way to answer these questions.

A New Province of Knowledge

In the next few pages, I will describe a revolution in human understanding. This revolution has been going on for about one hundred years; it harbors an enormous potential for improving human relations, indeed, human existence generally; it has catalyzed and continues to catalyze major changes in our private and public conduct both as children and adults; and finally, it allows us to discern the motivational dynamics not only of religious faith but of a great many other significant human behaviors. I am referring to the comprehensive study of infancy and childhood.

Until recently, babies were routinely operated upon without anesthetics because the doctors believed the babies did not feel pain. Astounding as that may seem, it is not untypical of the ignorance and insensitivity that Westerners have displayed toward infants over the centuries. If the reader has an appetite for this type of horror story, I refer him to the work of those psycho-historians who have been devoting themselves to the subject for several decades (see de Mause 1982). Although the mistreatment of babies is still a common occurrence, and may always be common given the tendency of people to transfer their frustrations and discontentments to their offspring, we are at last beginning to grasp in some depth what might be called the nature of the infant's special world.

It will be my contention in this chapter, as it is my contention in this book, that we cannot comprehend the religious realm apart from this new and revolutionary knowledge. Unless we are willing to view religion as addressing, or attempting to resolve, the dilemmas of infancy and childhood, we will simply miss out. Our understanding will not merely be partial; it will be hopelessly flawed, hopelessly incomplete. That is the nature of genuine revolutions; they change perceptions, and they leave behind those who are unable or unwilling to have their perceptions changed.

Psychoanalysis was instrumentally bound up, of course, with the advent of this revolution, and because psychoanalysis was a new discipline with huge and difficult territories to chart, and many original minds were involved in the charting, the revolution went forward amidst considerable

controversy. Although Freud made important contributions to the understanding of infantile sexuality and narcissism, his own personal resistance
to the study of the mother-infant bond, as well as his preoccupation with
the Oedipus complex (the second resulted in some measure from the first),
discouraged investigators from examining meticulously the psychological
realities of the early period. However, by the 1930s through the pioneering
work of Melanie Klein and her followers, and by the 1950s through the
work of Winnicott, Fairbairn, and Bowlby, significant and permanent in-
roads were being made into this new province of knowledge. People were
beginning to appreciate in earnest the degree to which the mind and the
emotions are shaped, even determined, by the original relationship between the parent and the child.

I am not suggesting that controversy ceased after Freud's resistances
were skirted. There was still disagreement, and there will always be disagreement given the problematical nature of the subject and the difficulty
of devising so-called objective measures. Does the relation between mother
and infant govern the nature and growth of the instinctual endowment?
Can what psychoanalysis calls instinct theory be reconciled with what it
calls object relations theory? Are there instincts at all in any true sense of the
word? What is the father's role during the formative years? And what
about changing patterns of infant care? Such questions are raised routinely
in a variety of psychoanalytic publications; obviously, we are not going to
resolve them here once and for all. What we can underscore, however, is
that by the present day a remarkable consensus has emerged on the importance of merger and separation as a key psychological conflict of the early
period.

Regardless of the geographical location and the nature of familial organization, the conflict between separation and merger not only dominates
the life of the infant but extends itself far beyond infancy and childhood
into the life of the adolescent and adult. It revolves around the struggle to
become an autonomous, separate person, differentiated and distinct, and
at the same time, to retain one's connection to significant others—either the
actual parents or their later substitutes in a protean variety of shapes and
forms. For the human creature, two of life's most powerful needs are, paradoxically, to be joined and to be separate, to be related and to be independent, to be autonomous and to be connected, and it is precisely this
paradoxical and in some sense contradictory thrust in human growth and
development, this antithetical, two-sided inclination of people, that makes
human behavior so problematical, so maddeningly difficult to see and to
fathom, and that brings so much confusion to the lives of individuals and
societies. Ethel Person, in her wonderful book *Dreams of Love and Fateful En-*

counters (1990, 132), renders the matter this way: "Without self-will there can be no psychological separation. But neither is there any highly individuated self. The self is delineated only through separation, but the sense of being separated proves impossible to bear. The solitary self feels cut off, alone, without resources. The solitary self feels impelled to merge with new object." What Dr. Person has captured, if I may be permitted to indicate the issue still again, is that the two needs—to be separate and joined, independent and connected—are, from a deep psychological angle, one need neither side of which finds expression without engaging the other, like a crab going backward and forward at the same time. When the desire for merger is felt, it typically engages the need to be separate, and the need to be separate engages the wish to be connected, joined. While it is easy to write about the matter, to employ such terms as alogical, paradoxical, and antithetical, it can be most unpleasant to experience the actual conflict when it occurs, along with the inner confusion that it often engenders. I would suggest, in fact, that we have here a major source of human stress.

From the many psychoanalytic accounts of infancy and childhood and of the growth and development of the human creature, I choose what is generally regarded as the most methodologically sophisticated, accurate, and helpful, namely, Margaret Mahler's *Psychological Birth of the Human Infant* (1975).[2] A child psychiatrist and pediatrician working with normal children in a specially constructed facility in New York City during the 1950s and 1960s, Mahler (and her associates) places the accent immediately on the struggle between separation and union.

We take for granted, she reminds us (3), our experience of ourselves as both fully "in" and fully separate from the "world out there." Our consciousness of ourselves as distinct, differentiated entities and our concomitant absorption into the external environment, without an awareness of self, are the polarities between which we move with varying ease, and with varying degrees of alternation or simultaneity. Yet the establishment of such consciousness, such ordinary, taken-for-granted awareness, is a slowly unfolding process that is not coincident in time with our biological emergence from the womb. It is tied closely and developmentally to our dawning experience of our bodies as separate in space and belonging only to us, and to our dawning experience of the primary love object as also separate in space, as having an existence of her/his own. Moreover, the struggle to achieve this individuation reverberates throughout the course of our lives: "It is never finished; it remains always active; new phases of the life cycle find new derivatives of the earliest processes still at work" (3). As we shall see, the realm of prayer is designed in large measure to address the endless transformations of these "early processes."

What must be stressed in particular here is the strength of both sides of the polarity. Children, with every move toward maturation, are confronted with the threat of "object loss," with traumatic situations involving separation from the caregiver. Thus they are constantly tempted to draw back, to regress, to move toward the object and the old relation as opposed to away from the object and the anticipated future, the new reality. At the same time, the normally endowed child strives mightily to emerge from his early fusion (we could say confusion) with the mother, to escape and to grow. His individuation consists precisely of those developmental achievements, those increasing motor and mental accomplishments, that begin to mark his separate existence, his separate identity as a separate being. The ambivalent impulses toward and away from the object, the great urge to differentiate and at the same time stay connected, are in Mahler's words, forever intertwined (4), although they may proceed divergently, one or the other lagging behind or leaping ahead during a given period.

Mahler makes plain that this process is not merely one of many equally important processes which transpire during the early time. On the contrary, the achievement of separation constitutes the very core of the self (4), the foundation of one's identity and being as a person. Yet this foundation can be gained (and here is the echo of a paradox again) only if the parent gives to the child a persistent, uninterrupted feeling of connection, of union—a tie that encourages the very breaking of it. This delicate balancing act is never perfect, and Mahler emphasizes throughout the course of her study that old conflicts over separation, old, unresolved issues of identity and bodily boundaries, can be reawakened or even remain active throughout the course of one's existence, at any or all stages of the life cycle. What appears to be a struggle for connection or distinctness in the now of one's experience can be the flare up of the ancient struggle in which one's self began to emerge from the orbit of the *magna mater*. We will shortly be exploring the degree to which this last observation sheds light upon one facet of prayer in which the practitioner longs to be absorbed into the supernatural body of the Deity.

By separation, then, Mahler does not mean primarily the physical separation of the baby in space or the distance from the caregiver, the kind of separation we associate, for example, with the work of John Bowlby. What Mahler has in mind is an inward or intrapsychic separation from both the mother and her extension, the world. The gradual development of this subjective awareness, this inward perception of the self and the other, leads eventually to clear, distinct inner representations of a "self" which is distinguished from "external objects." It is precisely this sense of being a separate individual that psychotic children are unable to achieve.

Similarly, when Mahler uses the term *symbiosis*, the accent is not upon a behavioral state but an inward condition, a feature of primitive emotional life wherein the differentiation between the self and the mother has not occurred, or where a regression to an undifferentiated state has occurred. This does not necessarily require the presence of the mother; it can be based on primitive images of oneness, or on a denial of perceptions that postulate separation. Thus for Mahler, identity during the early period does not refer to the child having a sense of who he is; it refers to the child having a sense *that* he is (8). Indeed, the sense that he is can be regarded as the first step in the process of an unfolding individuality. The achievement of separation-individuation is a kind of "second birth," a "hatching" (9) from the symbiotic mother-infant "membrane" in which the child is originally contained.

The Stages of Development

Mahler calls the earliest stage of development "autistic." The infant "spends most of his day in a half-sleeping, half-waking state" (41). He awakens mainly to feed and falls to sleep again when he is satisfied, or relieved of tensions. "Physiological rather than psychological processes are dominant," and the period as a whole is "best seen" in physiological terms. There is nothing abnormal about this "autism," as Mahler employs the term. The baby simply lacks awareness of the mother as a ministering agent and of himself as the object of her ministrations.[3]

From the second month on, however, the baby increasingly feels the presence of the mother, and it is just this sense of the caretaker (or the "need-satisfying object") being there that marks the inception of the normal symbiotic phase, which reaches a peak of intensity at about six to nine months. The most remarkable feature of this phase (and one that will be of great significance for us as we proceed with our study of prayer) is contained in Mahler's point that the infant "behaves and functions as though he and his mother were an omnipotent system—a dual unity with one common boundary" (44). The symbiotic infant participates emotionally and perceptually in a kind of delusional or hallucinatory fusion with the omnipotent mothering figure. Later in infancy and childhood, and indeed later in life at all stages when we experience severe stress, "this is the mechanism to which the ego regresses." Mahler hypothesizes that the symbiotic stage is "perhaps what Freud and Romain Rolland discussed in their dialogue as the sense of boundlessness of the oceanic feeling" (44). Psychoanalytic discussions of religion, and in particular of mystical states, generally begin with a reference to the Freud-Rolland exchange (see Freud [1930] 1961, 11).

In this way, when the autistic phase subsides, or, to use the metaphors characteristic of Mahler's treatise, when the "autistic shell" has "cracked" and the child can no longer "keep out external stimuli," a "second protective, yet selective and receptive shield" begins to develop in the form of the "symbiotic orbit," the mother and the child's dual-unity. While the normal autistic phase serves postnatal physiological growth and homeostasis, the normal symbiotic phase marks the all-important human capacity to bring the mother into a psychic fusion that comprises "the primal soil from which *all subsequent relationships form*" (48; my emphasis). We commence our existence as people in the illusion that the other (who appears to be omnipotent) is a part of the self. Although the mother is actually out there, ministering to the child, she is perceived by the latter to be a facet of his own organism, his own primitive ego. What the mother "magically" accomplishes in the way of care—the production of milk, the provision of warmth, the sensation of security—the baby omnipotently attributes to the mother and to himself. At the emotional, preverbal level, he declares, in effect, "I am not separate from my symbiotic partner; my partner and I are one. Whatever my partner appears to possess and to do, I possess and do as well. Whatever power my partner has, I also have. We are one, one omnipotent indestructible unit, twin stars revolving around each other in a single orbit of emotion and will." As D. W. Winnicott (1974, 13) unforgettably expresses it, the feeling of omnipotence is so strong in the infant (and so persistently clung to in the growing child when the dual-unity of the symbiotic stage begins to break down) that it is "nearly a fact." What this means, of course, is that the decline of symbiosis, or the increasing awareness of separation on the part of the child, will be experienced as a loss of self. If union with mother means wholeness, then dis-union will mean less than wholeness. As Mahler phrases it elsewhere (1968, 9), the cessation of the symbiotic phase marks the "loss of a part of [one's] ego." Let us examine Mahler's account of this original human trauma (the expulsion from paradise), and let us bear in mind as we proceed, first, that the transition from symbiosis to individuation is a multifaceted, complex process that consumes the first three years of life, and second, that for many, many people the loss of omnipotent merger and the narcissistic gratification that goes with it is never entirely accepted at the deep, unconscious level. I am not suggesting that the infant's growing abilities and independence fail to provide him with satisfaction; to be sure, they do, and Mahler is careful to emphasize both sides of the equation—the drive to remain with and to relinquish the mother. I am suggesting only that the movement away is attended by powerful anxiety and by the irrational wish to have it both ways: separateness and symbiotic union. Also, as one would suspect, the babies in Mahler's study often differ dramatically in their developmental inclinations and capacities, but more of that later.

Separation under Way

What Mahler calls the first subphase of differentiation occurs "at the peak of symbiosis" when the infant is about six months old. During his more frequent periods of wakefulness, the field of his attention gradually expands "through the coming into being of outwardly directed perceptual activity" (53). No longer is the "symbiotic orbit" the exclusive focus of his limited, yet evolving "sensorium." In addition, the baby's attention gradually combines with "a growing store of memories of mother's comings and goings, of good and bad experiences" which comprise the mnemonic core of what psychoanalysis call the "good" and the "bad" object. The infant is more alert, more goal-directed, and his attendants begin to talk of his "hatching," of his emergence from the "autistic shell."

As the seventh month approaches, "there are definite signs that the baby is beginning to differentiate his own body" from that of his mother (54). "Tentative experimentation at individuation" can be observed in such behavior as "pulling at the mother's hair, ears, or nose, putting food into the mother's mouth, and straining his body away from mother in order to have a better look at her, to scan her and the environment. This is in contrast to simply moulding into mother when held." The infant's growing visual and motor powers help him to "draw his body together" (55) and to commence the construction of his own, separate ego on the basis of this bodily awareness and sensation. At times, the baby even begins to move away from the mother's enveloping arms, to resist the passive "lap babyhood" which marks the earliest months of life. As he does this, however, he constantly checks back to mother with his eyes. He is becoming interested in mother as mother and compares her with other people and things. He discovers what belongs and what does not belong to the mother's body—a brooch, eyeglasses, a comb. He is starting to discriminate, in short, between the mother and all that which is different from or similar to her.

This early experiment in individuation on the baby's part is accompanied by considerable anxiety, the most striking manifestation of which occurs in the presence of strangers. Like so much else in the area of separation-union, stranger anxiety evinces two distinct yet interrelated aspects. On the one hand, strangers fascinate the infant, who, in Mahler's words, shows great "eagerness to find out about them" (56). On the other hand, strangers terrify the infant by reminding him of the other-than-mother world, the world of separation, the world that appears as symbiosis and dual-unity fade. After pointing out that babies vary in their susceptibility to stranger anxiety (and other anxiety as well), Mahler offers us the example of Peter, who at eight months reacts initially with wonder and curiosity to a stranger's mild overtures for his attention. Yet, two minutes later, although he is close to his mother, even leaning against her leg, Peter bursts into tears as the stranger touches his hair (57). Such is the emotional turbulence that accompanies the onset of individuation during the first subphase.

Increasing Autonomy, Persistent Ambivalence

Mahler divides the second subphase into the early practicing period and the practicing subphase proper. During the former, the ten- to eleven-month infant becomes more and more deeply absorbed in his expanding mental and physical universe. He begins rapidly to distinguish his own body from his mother's, to actively establish a specific (as opposed to symbiotic) bond with her, and to indulge his autonomous, independent interests while in close proximity to her. In a word, he begins to transfer his absorption in mother to the world around him. He explores the objects in his vicinity—toys, bottles, blankets—with his eyes, hands, and mouth; his growing locomotor capacity widens his environment. Not only does he have a "more active role in determining closeness and distance to mother," but the "modalities that up to now were used to explore the relatively familiar" suddenly transport him to a new reality. There is more to see, to hear, to touch (66).

Yet in all of this, Mahler is careful to point out, the mother is "still the center of the child's universe" (66). His experience of his "new world" "is subtly related" to her, and his excursions into the other-than-mother realm are often followed by periods of intense clinging and a refusal to separate. For an interval the baby is absorbed in some external object and seems oblivious to mother's presence; a moment later he jumps up and rushes to her side expressing his need for physical proximity. Again and again he displays a desire for "emotional refueling" (69), that is to say, for a dose of maternal supplies—hugging, stroking, chatting—after a period of independent activity. What Mahler's children (and all children) want—and we come here to a crucial utterance—is to "move away independently" from the mother and, at the same time, to "remain connected to her" (70).

The practicing subphase proper (eleven to fifteen months) marks the high point of the child's move toward a separate existence. Not only does he experience a dramatic spurt in cognitive development, he also achieves what Mahler calls "the greatest step in human individuation," his upright locomotion (71). These "precious months" of increasing powers and skills comprise "the child's love affair with the world": the "plane of his vision changes; . . . he finds unexpected and changing perspectives. . . . The world is the junior toddler's oyster. . . . Narcissism is at its peak. . . . The chief characteristic of this period is the child's great narcissistic investment in his own functions, his own body, and the objectives of his expanding reality" (71). Adding to the exhilaration, notes Mahler, is the child's "elated escape from fusion with, from engulfment by, mother." Here is the movement away in its most striking biological and psychological expression.

Yet even here, in the midst of this great expansion, this "love affair with the world," the paradoxical, ambivalent aspect of human development rears its head as mightily as ever in the form of deep-seated, pervasive anxiety. "The course of true love never did run smooth," observes Shakespeare, and the words would seem to apply to our earliest developmental experiences. The child's rapidly expanding ego functions bring with them both the threat of object loss and the fear of being reengulfed by the mother. One minute he expresses a need for checking back, for emotional refueling, for knowing exactly the mother's whereabouts; the next minute he forcibly removes himself from mother's caressing arms in an effort to assert his capacity for active, independent functioning. Sometimes the baby runs away to make sure mother wants to catch him up; yet when she does, he shows resentment at being held and stroked.

Even the enormous step of upright locomotion and the increase in perception that it brings to the child holds both sides of the dual-unity equation. It is the need for mother's emotional support at the instant he learns to walk that Mahler captures unforgettably: "The child walks alone with his eyes fixed on his mother's face, not on the difficulties in his way. . . . In the very same moment that he is emphasizing his need for her, he is proving that he can do without her." In this way, the toddler "feels the pull of separation from his mother at the same time he asserts his individuation. It is a *mixed* experience, the child demonstrating that he can and cannot do without his mother" (73; my emphasis). As for the mother's physical absence during this period (she may be working, ill, etc.), it typically sparks sadness, or even depression, in the infant. The symbiotic mothering half of the self is missed during the very subphase that is most obviously filled with the joys of separation (74).

Undeniably Alone

The entire separation-individuation process culminates at approximately thirty months in what Mahler terms "the rapprochement subphase," the period during which the infant perceives with growing clarity and certainty that he and mother are separate beings, that the old symbiosis and the narcissistic gratifications (including omnipotence) that go with it are illusory, that he is physically and psychically alone. Here is Mahler's (78) powerful description of this watershed in a person's life: "With the acquisition of primitive skills and perceptual cognitive faculties there has been an increasingly clear differentiation, a separation, between the intrapsychic representation of the object and the self-representation. At the very height of mastery, toward the end of the practicing period, it had already begun to dawn on the junior toddler that the world is not his oyster, that he must cope with it more or less on his own, very often as a relatively helpless, small, and separate individual, unable to command relief or assistance merely by feeling the need for it or by giving voice to that need" (omnipotence). We may note parenthetically at this juncture, that much magical and religious activity is designed to deny precisely this momentous event, and not only deny it but bring about its reversal through just those mechanisms that Mahler mentions here, namely, "mere feeling" (wishing) and "giving voice" (prayers and invocations). During the course of the next chapter we will explore these denials and reversals in great depth.

With the erosion of symbiosis, the "fear of losing the *love* of the object" (78), as opposed to losing the object, makes itself felt increasingly in the child. Up to this point (the rapprochement subphase) the object and the self have been more or less psychically indistinguishable. Now, as differentiation occurs in earnest, the object's love becomes the focus of the child's attention. This does not mean that the original anxiety over loss of the object as a part of the self disappears. It means only that an additional, more conscious or even cognitive anxiety has been superimposed upon the original, primal dread. Accordingly, the toddler begins to demand the mother's constant attention. He is deeply preoccupied with her whereabouts. He expresses enormous anger and anxiety at her leave-taking and anguish at being left behind. He clings to mother, seeks her lap, and may begin to show a dependent interest in maternal substitutes. In a thousand ways he attempts to coerce the mother into fulfilling his wishes. He tries at times to be magnificently separate, omnipotent, rejecting: he will gain the mother's love and attention by showing her the proverbial cold shoulder. At other times he plays the helpless baby. For weeks on end his wooing of mother alternates sharply with his expressions of resentment and outrage (97).

How do the mothers react to all this? "Some cannot accept the child's demandingness; others are unable to face the child's gradual separation, the fact that the child can no longer be regarded as part of her" (78). Yet, whatever the relational dynamics happen to be, they cannot stop the process: "no matter how insistently the toddler tries to coerce the mother, she and he can no longer function effectively as a dual unit—that is to say, the child can no longer maintain his delusion of parental omnipotence, which he still at times expects will restore the symbiotic status quo." The child must "gradually and painfully give up the delusion of his own grandeur, often by way of dramatic fights with mother—less so, it seemed to us, with father. This is the crossroads of what we term the rapprochement crisis" (79). Mahler observes in a sentence at which we prick up our ears as we near the study of the supernatural that "many uniquely human problems and dilemmas" which are "sometimes never completely resolved during the entire life cycle" have their origin here, during the end of symbiosis and the onset of separation (100).

Resolving the Dilemma

The resolution of the rapprochement crisis comes about in a variety of ways, the description of which concludes the first half of Mahler's study. As the child experiences a growing capacity to be alone, his clamoring for omnipotent control starts to diminish. He shows less separation anxiety, fewer alternating demands for closeness and autonomy. Not only does he begin to understand empathetically what his mother is going through, which allows him to "unify the good and bad objects into one whole representation" (110), but he begins to identify with the problems and struggles of the youngsters around him. In this way, he begins to turn to other people, and in many instances to his own father, in his effort to satisfy his needs. And with the wholesale emergence of gender differences, he starts to participate in those activities that are peculiar to his/her sex.

Equally important, the child's capacity for verbalization and symbolization begins to lead him toward the cultural realm, toward an endless variety of substitutive, or, in Winnicott's (1971, 188) famous expression, "transitional" objects that characteristically take the form of "blankies," storybooks, toys, pets, and so on, and that exist somewhere "between the child's fantasies and reality," in what Winnicott calls "transitional space." We might say that the child's growing ability to incorporate the world into his burgeoning ego leads him to a series of new internalizations, new inward presences, which are appropriate to his age and to the problems he confronts. He is beginning to live with his own thoughts and with the companions of his inner world. This is what we usually mean by being alone.

In the majority of cases and generally for all normal children, such developments culminate in the establishment of what Mahler calls object constancy (110), and with it, the inception of an individuated life. By object constancy Mahler has in mind "the presence of a reliable internal image that remains relatively stable irrespective of the state of instinctual need or inner discomfort. On the basis of this achievement, temporary separation can be lengthened and better tolerated" (110). This is the necessary step, the vital inward accomplishment, that permits further growth, further individuation, and further ego strength in the preschooler and eventually in the school child.

Mahler devotes the second half of her treatise to several lengthy case histories in which we see children struggling from normal autism and symbiosis to separation and individuation. She strives in these sections to illustrate her theoretical position at the clinical level, the level from which the theoretical materials originally arose, of course. As she does this, Mahler makes clear something that she stresses in many places in part 1, namely that it is the combination of a particular caretaker interacting with a particular child that ultimately shapes the child's emerging character in terms of both conscious and unconscious processes. Projections pass not only from the baby to the mother, but from the mother to the baby as well. "It seemed that the ability to cope with separateness, as well as with actual physical separation," declares Mahler (103), "was dependent in each case on the history of the mother-child relationship, as well as on its present state. We found it hard to pinpoint just what it was in the individual cases that produced more anxiety in some and an ability to cope in others. Each child had established by this time his own characteristic ways of coping." Thus, when we look at the whole picture, we spy an element of mystery, a unique, intangible quality that pertains to each mother-infant bond and that can never be fully explained by observers, or indeed by the mother and infant who are involved in the relationship. What occurs early on is not strictly an enigma but it has its enigmatic aspect, and we must always bear this in mind. Human behavior finally escapes whatever logical space we try to fit it into. Reality happens, from the inside, and can never be perfectly reconstructed.

As I suggested on several occasions in the context, the struggle for and against separation extends itself powerfully not only into ritualistic behaviors such as prayer but into the nature and development of our perceptual lives generally, including the whole of culture. Although it may appear a bit strange to express the matter thus, our ordinary consciousness in the widest, most all-inclusive sense is inextricably bound up with the early struggle over separation and cannot be grasped apart from it. We must remember as we move through the next few pages that what Mahler describes in the final paragraphs of her theoretical section is the passing of the rapprochement crises, not the passing of the separation-union conflict. Indeed, it is the thesis of this book, and has been from the outset, that this conflict never ceases, that it so forcefully shapes and directs our conduct as to gain a place among the central conflicts of our experience as a form of life.

As Mahler herself makes clear (115), a "sound image" of the maternal figure does not mean that the old longing for merger stops, that the fear of reengulfment goes away, that anxiety, ambivalence, and splitting suddenly vanish, along with feelings of omnipotence and narcissistic grandiosity; it does not mean that the primal terrors of rejection and loss miraculously disappear forever. The establishment of a sound maternal image simply means that the little person can stumble ahead still loaded with the great, absorbing issues of the early time, still loaded with the stress that attends the erosion of symbiosis, still wishing contradictorily for both merger and differentiation, and still smarting from the collapse of dual-unity. What occurs as the infant undergoes separation has been described by Rizzuto (1979, 49) as a "life-long mourning process that triggers an endless search for replacement." To express the matter from a different yet crucially related angle, the passing of the rapprochement crisis simply means that one is now in a position to act out among others this basic human dilemma, this rooted, unconscious issue as it manifests itself projectively at the levels of both individual and group conduct. It means that one can now seek for omnipotence, fusion, and narcissistic gratification in the wider world. In a manner of speaking, one is loose. Hopefully, the old cliché that we are more or less neurotic emerges with fresh clarity at this juncture.

Let us deepen and enrich Mahler's findings, then, and conclude our psychoanalytic investigation of origins, by concentrating once more on the first years of life, this time with ordinary consciousness itself as the focus.

PART TWO

Construction of the Inner Realm

It boils down to this: From the beginning of our existence we internalize the world; we take experiential events into our emerging mind-body, and we do this fully, deeply, and finally at the level of ganglionic-synaptic development itself. If the reader is wondering why the early period is so crucial, so all-determining for our later lives, this is where the answer begins to emerge, in the psychodynamics of human internalization. "Mind is born early in life," writes José Delgado (1971, 26), "as an infant is attracted to sources of comfort and repelled by sources of distress." Even when we are thinking logically as adults, even when we are indulging in the pure reason that we associate with philosophers such as Descartes and Kant, the legacy of our early years is there, humming beneath the surface, as it were. If one can think of the multifaceted human ego as a group of actors standing on a stage, one will understand pure reason as a mental request that everyone move out of the way so that reason may preside at the center. The cooperative members of the cast may do this, but they do not leave the stage, and they influence reason by their continued presence there. The living organism, in other words, always perceives the world with the whole mind, as opposed to thinking about it with only a part of the mind. Perception, not thought, is primary. This also holds for regression. I mean, when adults regress amidst crisis, or when they become involved in childlike activities, they do not generally regress altogether. Parts or aspects of the personality remain at appropriately mature levels. Again, perception as a whole, not thought, is primary (see Blum 1994, 73).

Of the powerful internalizing that we do toward the inception of our lives, that which involves the caretaker (usually the mother) is of enormous significance. As developmental psychologists express it, the object (this term is used, remember, because the caretaker is not yet perceived by the baby as a person) "enters the infant's dawning psyche" as the deep internalization of life's earliest phase, and she "persists there as a presence, later to become an image" during the period in which verbalization begins. This interplay between mother and infant is "directly involved in the shaping of the infant's personality." Intuitive or feeling perception "begins with maximal intensity at birth as the baby becomes subject in a structuring way to the maternal attitude" (Rheingold 1964, 30). So intense, so pervasive, and so basic is this interaction between mother and child that we would do well to regard the mother herself not as a distinct entity but as a kind of organ of the baby. It is in the growth of this unique union, or in the evolution of this unique "biological state" (Gallagher 1992, 13), that we find the nucleus of human identity.

The Mirror

The genesis and the formation of the self derive from the baby's initial mirroring experience with the mother. For the past few decades this remarkable aspect of our origins has been studied intensively and has come to be regarded as a central feature of our development. The investigations of René Spitz (1965, 81) and his associates during the 1950s and 1960s established at the clinical level the baby's inclination to concentrate on the mother's face—and in particular on her eyes—during periods of feeding. For three, or perhaps four, months the nursing infant does not look at the mother's breast (or at the bottle held close to her breast) but at her face. "From the moment the mother comes into the room to the end of nursing he stares at her face." What is especially interesting in this regard is the connection between such primal gazing and the mouth, or oral cavity.

While the child takes into his mouth and body his physical nourishment, he takes into his dawning awareness or his visceral brain the emotional, psychological materials that he discovers in the face, eyes, and bodily attitude of the mother. It is often remarked that the first ego is a body ego and that our later life is influenced at the perceptual level by the foundational experiences our bodies undergo as consciousness awakens. We have here a compelling instance of how this works. When Spitz calls the oral cavity in its conjunction with the mother's body "the cradle of human perception," he reminds us that sucking in and spitting out are the first, the most basic, and the most persistent perceptual behaviors among humans. They underlie at the bodily level our subsequent rejections and acceptances, our subsequent negations and celebrations, of experience.

Although Spitz established the baby's inclination to stare at the mother's face, notes H. M. Southwood (1973, 235–39), whose discussion I will follow closely here, he did not state that mother and infant spend considerable time looking at each other, nor did he contend that such looking, along with the mother initiating the infant's facial expressions and sounds, provided the means for the baby to regard the mother's face and sounds as his own. An inborn tendency on the part of the infant prompts him to seek out his mother's gaze and to do so regularly and for extended periods. The mother, because of tendencies developed during the course of her relationship with her own mother, sets about exploiting this mutual face-gazing activity. As the eye-to-eye contact becomes frequent, and easily observed by the investigator, the mother's inclination to continually change her facial expression, as well as the quality of her vocalizing, emerges with striking clarity. Usually she smiles and nods and coos; sometimes in response to an infant frown she frowns. In virtually every instance the mother's facial and vocal behavior comprises an imitation of the baby's.

Thus, as the mother descends to the infant's level, she provides him with a particular kind of human reflection. She does not simply give the baby back his own self; she reinforces a portion of the baby's behavior in comparison with another portion. She gives the baby back not merely a part of what he is doing but something of her own in addition. In individual development, "the precursor of the mirror is the mother's face" (Winnicott 1971, 130). The upshot may be stated as follows: the kind of behavior we connect with the ego or the perceptual apparatus derives in large measure from the behavior of the mother. Not only does she trigger the ego's formation, she determines the kind of stimuli to which the child will attend, including the stimuli that will eventually come through language.

Our mental makeup, then, is shaped by those with whom we entered into object relations during the early phases of our development. Our earliest objects become dynamic parts of our personality structure and continue to influence us in all that we do long after the specific persons who were the aim of our internalizing tendency have ceased to be. By the time we have reached adulthood, there exists within us an inner world, a kind of psychic universe which is inhabited by the objects that have entered us, or more properly, that we have taken into ourselves along our maturational way. We live in two worlds, from the beginning, and our perceptual life must be regarded as a function of the interaction of these worlds which continually impinge upon one another.

The Dark Side of the Mirror: Splitting

We are beginning to understand the psychological direction from which our ordinary awareness arises. To do this more fully, however, we must grasp the two-sided, or split nature of our early, foundational experience, something that Mahler touched upon during the course of her investigations.

On the one hand, many of the representational units which the baby takes in contribute to his contentment. The mother gives him a positive, nurturing introduction to existence. She soothes him, reassures him, delights him; she develops his confidence, his enthusiasm, his joy in life. In a word, she triggers his participation in good materials. On the other hand, many of the units that are assimilated by the growing child are disruptive, or, in a very special sense, negative in quality.

As the child goes about building up his good maternal representation, as he gradually enlarges those aspects of the caretaker that will serve as the perceptual basis for his positive participation in the world, he confronts of necessity the imperfections of the symbiotic relationship in which he is involved. No matter how solicitous the mother is, the infant is fated to undergo tension, frustration, discomfort, and even a certain amount of pain. Such experiences mobilize anxiety. Indeed, very young infants display identical patters of anxious behavior when they are in contact with the caretaker during a period in which she is tense, angry, disquieted, or anxious herself. Repeated, inescapable exposure to inconsistent conduct prompts the developing baby to split the caretaker into a "good" and a "bad object" and to internalize these objects into a part or aspect of his perceiving self. The collection of people which each of us harbors within, carries about, and projects into our reality, reaches back in every instance to the first pair of our personifications: the good mother and the bad or evil mother. With the passage of time these early, primitive personifications get transmuted into the good me, the bad me, and the ambiguous, dreadful not me (Rheingold 1964, 164).

We must remember here that the mother's inconsistency is a grave, disruptive event for the child, that it corresponds to his worst imaginings and fears. The postponement of gratification from its mother's supplies constitutes for the infant a trauma, and residues of the infant's reaction to this trauma can be found in the psychology of later years. Because he is simply not able to integrate the mother's two sides, her "bad" and "good" aspects, the infant attempts to coordinate them by splitting and then dealing with the splits. He declares, in effect, "*Mother* is not bad. There just happens to be this bad mother who appears once in a while. She and mother are not really the same person, for *mother* is always good and will never hurt and disappoint. I am obliged to interact with both *mother* and the other one." Only later, when the child achieves object constancy, will he be able to accept goodness and badness in the same person (see Parker 1995, 174).

Thus, threats to our narcissistic integrity, to our primitive emotional and bodily self-esteem, exist from the inception of our psychic lives and stem from the interaction of the child's wishes and needs with the demands and frustrations of the external world. Such narcissistic wounds may evoke feelings of depression and a growing sense of perplexity, which is frequently answered with aggressive behavior. The infant's mere inability to influence, predict, or comprehend an event, which he expected on the basis of his previous experience to be able to control or understand, is registered as trauma. Because the infant's thought, the whole of his primitive mentation, is tied inextricably to the mother, her mere absence through temporary departure can leave the infant with the terrible feeling that he is empty, empty in his mind and emotions. We may have here the deep origin and most basic, enduring expression of the feeling that one is "losing one's mind." We also now realize that the parent's very power over the life and death of the child is perceived as threatening and internalized to become part of everyone's susceptibility to nightmare, everyone's residual paranoia. Odd as it may sound to express it this way, merely being born human is a major source of stress. In the words of Michael Eigen (1985, 329), "fragmentation and division are as much a part of our starting point as union and continuity."

The Jungian research of Erich Neumann (1970, 148) are helpful on this score. The symbolism of the "Terrible Mother," he writes, "draws its images from the inside," that is, the bad object appears in fantastic, ghastly forms that do not originate in the environment. Whether we are in "Egypt or India, Mexico or Etruria, Bali or Rome," we confront the archetypal expression of these intrapsychic "monsters." In the tales and myths of "all peoples, ages, and countries," as well as in our own nightmares, "witches, vampires, ghouls and spectres assail us, all terrifyingly alike." It is the internalizing of this bad object that explains our emotional fear of death. At issue here is not death as the adult conceives it, but a threat of a quality and magnitude beyond the adult's imagination. We get a glimpse of it in states of panic and in the momentary probe into infancy that some individuals experience during the course of psychotherapy (Rheingold 1964). Thus the struggle between the forces of life and death, which is inherent in the biologically precarious infantile condition, becomes involved in the infant's response to the mother that protects and satisfies and to the mother that frustrates and deprives. Where the fear of death is concerned, it is the uncertain ties to the living world at all ages that shake us more than the awareness of biological cessation (Steinzor 1979).

What I am maintaining is that we cannot understand the complex symbol that death comprises for the human creature, or the powerful role of death-consciousness in the impulse toward religious belief, if we exclude from the discussion the primal anxiety of the early period. "When a child has a fear of dying," writes Mary Shaw (1995, 141), "it often translates into an extreme fear of being separated from his mother." Because the mother's impact on the child is preverbal, because her presence is internalized before higher conceptualization begins, it is very, very difficult to subject our split foundations to reason. True, as Mahler points out, there is a diminution of splitting during the rapprochement subphase, when the child becomes more empathetic to the mother's position. But as I have suggested, this marks only a diminution (sometimes a temporary one) that permits the rapprochement crisis to pass. It does not even begin to mean that the human tendency towards splitting has ceased. On the contrary, our anxious obsession with death, as well as our dangerous indulgence in rigid, dichotomous views of the world, with the good guys over here and the bad guys over there, is rooted largely in the primitive splitting of the early time, which leaves perdurable traces on our normal perception.

Early Excitement, Early Affect

I want to reemphasize here that the parent-child interactions of the early period must not be viewed as primarily cognitive events. In the words of Daniel Stern (1985, 74–75), to whose *Interpersonal World of the Infant* I now turn, "they mainly involve affect and excitement" and become part of the infant's effort "to order the world by seeking invariants." When the preverbal, inward Representation of such Interaction becomes Generalized into what Stern calls a RIG, the infant's "sense of a core self" (90), or what we call the ego in previous sections, is well upon its developmental way. "Affects," writes Stern (89), "are excellent self-variants because of their relative fixity," which means, of course, that affects are a central part of mirroring. By creating a "continuity of experience" (90) and, in particular, a "continuity of *affective* experience" (93), the RIG provides the baby with the psychic, emotional foundation of his subsequent perceptual interactions with the world. As the Duke of Gloucester observes in Shakespeare's *King Lear*, we see the world "feelingly."

Thus mirroring in its early stages (we'll come to the later stages very soon) comprises for Stern (1985, 103) a mediation in which the caregiver "greatly influences the infant's sense of wonder and avidity for exploration." It is "only the feeling state" that belongs to the nascent self, that is a "self-invariant," and "merger experiences" become simply "a way of being with someone" (109). The infant lays down over and over again the memory of specific affective episodes; he/she develops RIGs; and he/she becomes susceptible to subsequent experiences that recall the foundational ones. Later affective exchanges reactivate the original exchanges; they "pack the wallop of the original lived experience in the form of an active memory" (110). This is the essence of the infant's affective world.

Evoked Companions

Employing terminology that will help us enormously in understanding prayer, Stern (1985, 116) calls these active memories "evoked companions" and suggests that they constitute what psychoanalysis usually refers to as internalized relationships. "For instance," Stern (113) writes in an effort to let us know exactly what he has in mind, "if a six-month-old, when alone, encounters a rattle and manages to grasp it and shake it so that it makes a sound, the initial pleasure may quickly become extreme delight and exuberance, expressed in smiling, vocalizing, and general body wriggling. The extreme delight and exuberance is not the only result of successful mastery, but also the historical result of similar past moments in the presence of a delight-and-exuberance-enhancing (regulating) other." It is partly a social response, but in this instance it takes place in a nonsocial situation. At such times, the original pleasure born of mastery acts as a retrieval cue and activates the RIG, resulting in an "imagined interaction with an evoked companion," which includes of course the "shared and mutually induced delight" about the mastery.

Equally crucial for our grasp of religious belief is Stern's (1985, 116) observation that evoked companions "never disappear." They "lie dormant throughout life," and while they are always retrievable, "their degree of activation is variable" (116). He writes, "various evoked companions will be almost constant companions in everyday life. Is it not so for adults when they are not occupied with tasks? How much time each day do we spend in imagined interactions that are either memories, or the fantasied practice of upcoming events, or daydreams?" (118) Robert Rogers (1991, 41) comments on these materials, "the seemingly unaccountable experience by an adult of strong emotion, such as love or anger, as a response to a relatively trivial situation involving a comparative stranger might be accounted for by assuming that an 'evoked companion' has suddenly been mobilized, however unconsciously. Where else could all that affect come from?" Thus "attachment is the internalized representation of repetitive interactions with caregivers" (1991, 41). What is internalized in the earliest representations "is not simply the infant's own action, nor the environments' response, but the dynamic interplay between the two" (1991, 41). Can anyone fail to spy here the manner in which these citations touch upon, indeed mesh with, our earlier discussion of separation anxiety as presented in Mahler?

Many individual and group behaviors and beliefs, particularly those that occur in the religious or spiritual realm, are designed unconsciously to address the problem of separation (and/or other psychological problems) by offering practitioners experiences that evoke companions. Such experiences grant the solace of companionship to those who are struggling in the after-separation-world, those whose aloneness, self-alienation, or persistent separation anxiety prime them to respond to an unseen universe of powerful forces and beings to which they are ostensibly connected. Indeed, many of the figures at the heart of religious ritual (God the Father, the Son, Mary, guardian angels) may be regarded in significant measure as projective, psychological expressions, or complex, multilayered symbolifications, of those longed-for inward companions associated originally with the dynamic affects included in the dual-unity situation, the baby's delicious, regulating, invariant and internalized encounters with the caregiving figures of the early period.

Affect Attunement

What Stern (1985, 124) calls "the next quantum leap in the sense of self" occurs when the infant discovers that he/she "has a mind and that other people have minds as well." Here we come to the first of two direct, foundational precursors of prayerful communion.

At about nine months, infants come gradually upon "the momentous realization" that subjective experiences are "potentially shareable with someone else." The infant "must arrive at a theory not only of separate minds but of interfaceable separate minds" (124). This is not, of course, a theory in the usual sense, but a "working notion that says something like, what is going on in my mind may be similar enough to what is going on in your mind that we can somehow communicate this without words and thereby experience intersubjectivity" (125). Now, intersubjective related-ness or the "new organizing subjective perspective about the self" is built upon a foundation of core relatedness, the sharing of affective states. Stern dubs this empathetic responsiveness between caregiver and child "affect attunement," observing that it comprises what is meant when clinicians speak of parental mirroring (138).

After presenting a wealth of clinical evidence for the existence of affect attunement, Stern (1985, 139) observes in a crucial passage:

> Strict imitation alone won't do. . . . The parent must be able to read the infant's feeling state from the infant's overt behavior, must perform some behavior that corresponds in some way to the infant's, and the infant must be able to read this parental response as having to do with his own original feeling.

Parent and infant are engaged in what we can term telepathic or clairvoy-ant exchanges; they manifest a kind of ESP in regard to affective states and affective wishes—what they want to happen as they interact on this inti-mate, feeling level. Stern (51) writes:

> Infants . . . appear to have an innate general capacity, which can be called *amodal* perception, to take information received in one sensory modality and somehow translate it into another sensory modality. We do not know how they accomplish this task. The information is prob-ably not experienced as belonging to any one particular sensory mode. More likely it transcends mode or channel and exists in some supra-modal form. . . . It involves an encoding into a still mysterious, amodal representation.

And again, what "the infant experiences are not sights and sounds and touches and namable objects, but rather shapes, intensities, and temporal patterns—the more 'global' qualities of experience" (51). And finally, "the experience of finding a cross-modal match . . . would feel like a correspon-dence or imbuing of present experience with something prior or familiar. Present experience would feel related in some way to experience from else-where" (52–53). Here we have a realistic, psychological source (through reactivation or unconscious memory) of what many consider to be the supernatural level upon which prayer transpires. Moreover—and perhaps of even greater importance—the essence of affect attunement between parent and child resides in its synchronous nature, in its happily timed interactive quality. Parent and offspring are affectively in synch. The parent knows intuitively, telepathically, clairvoyantly the affective meaning of the infant's signals, and the parent provides response in a timely fashion, magically echoing or mirroring the infant's inner world as the infant makes that world manifest. Conversely, the infant strives to engage the parent affectively in time to gratify his (the infant's) surging affect. Synchronous rapport, in short, is the pith of preverbal existence, and transaction takes place, says Stern (139), only when such conditions are met. Just as evoked companions never disappear, just as they lie dormant throughout life waiting to be activated, so affect attunements become deeply internalized, providing the emergent self with a foundational legacy of feeling that is sought over and over again in subsequent years. Indeed, it is attuning with vitality that permits us as humans to be with one another in the sense of sharing likely inner experiences on a continuous basis (157). Here is a memorable consequence: when we discover (or rediscover) an attunement, an evoked companion, an energetic, affective fix, we often feel transformed.

The Transformational Object

Guiding us toward the psychoanalytic heart of spiritual thinking, toward the essence of its interrelations with the early period, Christopher Bollas (1987, 13–14) observes in *The Shadow of the Object* that the infant's experience of his first object, the mother, is fundamentally transformative in character:

> It is undeniable that as the infant's other self, the mother transforms the baby's internal and external environment. . . . [She] is less significant and identifiable as an object than as a process that is identified with cumulative internal and external transformation.

Just as evoked companionship and affect attunement never disappear, so this feature of early existence "lives on in certain forms of object-seeking in adult life." The object is sought for its "function as a signifier of transformation." The quest is not to possess the object but to "surrender to it as a medium that alters the self," that promises to "transform the self" (14). It is an old refrain: having met you, or found Jesus, or joined the party, or started meditating, *I'm changed*. In significant measure, and in psychoanalytic terms, the refrain translates into something like this: I've rediscovered (through a degree of emotional regression) the transformational essence of the early period, of dual-unity, of mirroring. My new connection reunites me with a transforming internalized caretaker and thus diminishes my sense of separation. I am restored to the before-separation-world.

This conception of the maternal figure as transformational is supported by the overriding fact that she regularly alters the baby's environment to meet his needs; she "actually transforms his world" (Bollas 1987, 15). The infant identifies his own emerging capacities of motility, perception, and integration with the presence of the mother, and the failure of the mother to provide a facilitating environment can result in the ego's collapse. With the infant's creation of the transitional object (upon which I'll expand in a moment), the transformational process is "displaced from the mother- environment, where it originated, into countless subjective objects." The transitional phase is "heir to the transformational period." Not only can the infant play with the illusion of his omnipotence, he can experience the "freedom of metaphor" (15).

In a section titled "the search for the transformational object in adult life," Bollas (1987, 15) declares that psychoanalysis has failed to take notice of the "wide-ranging collective search for an object that is identified with the metamorphosis of the self." For example, in religious faith, when a person believes in the Deity's potential to transform the environment, he "sustains the terms of the earliest object tie within a mythic structure." Such knowledge is symbiotic (16), writes Bollas, touching implicitly on the theme of separation in Mahler. It (the symbiotic knowledge) "coexists alongside other forms of knowing." Esthetic objects, too, frequently elicit transformational response from the individual, who may feel a "deep subjective rapport" with a painting, poem, song, symphony, or landscape and experience "an uncanny fusion" with the item, an event that "re-evokes an ego state that prevailed during early psychic life" (16). Such occasions are "less noteworthy as transformational accomplishments" than they are for their "uncanny quality," the sense of being reminded of something "never cognitively apprehended but existentially known." They draw forth a sense of fusion, which is the individual's recollection of the transformational object. Thus, as psychological categories, transformation and separation are integrally related once again.

As I just suggested and wish to reemphasize here, the search for symbolic equivalents to the transformational object, and the experience with which it is identified, continues throughout the life cycle. We develop faith in a God whose absence is held ironically to be "as important a test of man's being as his presence" (Bollas 1987, 17). We visit the theater, the museum, the landscape of our choice, to "search for aesthetic experience." We may imagine the self "as the transformational facilitator," and we may invest ourselves with abilities to change the environment that are not only "impossible" but, upon reflection, "embarrassing" (17). In such daydreams, the self as transformational object is somewhere in the future, and even meditative planning about the future is often a "kind of psychic prayer for the arrival of the transformational object," a "secular second coming" of a relation experienced in the earliest period of life (17).

How does such transformation look during the early period? What are its phenomenological features? Here we reach the second direct, foundational precursor to prayerful communion, and in particular to divine intervention: God "answering" one's supplication. If the child is in "distress," writes Bollas (1987, 33), the "resolution of discomfort is achieved by the apparition-like presence of mother," who arrives in a timely, synchronous manner to remove the distress. Not only is the "pain of hunger" transformed "by mother's milk" into an experience of "fullness," but the transformation is accomplished synchronously, as the hungry child makes his needs known. Bollas calls this a "primary transformation": emptiness, agony, and anger become fullness and contentment. Over and over again during life's initial stages parent and offspring are joined in such ministering, synchronous encounters. The child is injured; the child cries out. Then what happens? The parent appears to soothe and "make better." The child is wet and uncomfortable; the child starts to squall. Then what happens? The parent appears with dry garments and ministering hands. In this way, the early period of maternal care comprises an endless series of "answered prayers." The big one, like a guardian angel, hovers over the little one and ministers to the little one's needs just as they arise. Of particular fascination here is the close, even inextricable connection between maternal care and the development of the time sense. The essentials of the matter are captured in a seminal paper by Hartocollis (1974, 243):

> As tension eases and the mother is not yet there the "good" object image or representation emerges protectively in fantasy and unites with the self-image in a need-fulfilling hallucinatory experience; but if the mother's arrival is further delayed, it begins to fade away rapidly. As the infant tries to hold onto it and unpleasure increases, the uncertain "good" object begins to turn into a "bad" one. It is the effort to hold onto the "good" object and expel the "bad" one that . . . creates the ability to anticipate the future.

Eventually what Hartocollis calls "object constancy" develops in the maturing child; the early hallucinatory process is replaced by the ability to anticipate the fulfillment of a need. As the fused good and bad maternal figures are set up within as the scaffolding for normal character development, a relatively trustful tendency to believe in good outcomes is projected onto the environment which begins to be experienced as continuous, as possessing the attribute of duration. Accordingly, the good object is in large measure good time, or synchronous attention and care. The bad object is, by contrast, delay and neglect. When we experience divine interventions in the now of our existence as adults, they are magical, powerful, "numinous" and convincing to the extent that they recall unconsciously the timely ministrations of the good, attentive parent. Indeed, such interventions can occur in the first place only because people tend to compartmentalize or split the parental object into its good and bad components, and people do this precisely as a consequence of the temporal side of their early care.

Let me sum the whole matter up from a slightly different angle. The Winnicottian moment of illusion, the foundation of religious belief, is specifically the moment of timely maternal ministration, the moment in which the maternal object transforms the infant's world, changing anxiety into security, discomfort into satisfaction. When the helpless little one cries out (proto-prayer), the omnipotent, caring big one (proto-deity) arrives to succor and to reassure. Remember, during life's first years this happens over and over again, thousands of times, and establishes for the child through simple conditioning the essential nature of reality. Accordingly, religious faith is the adult's wishful, willful insistence (based on experience) that the attentive caregiver of the early period is still there watching over one, that one's cry (prayer) can still beget the wished-for, loving, interventional response. To turn the coin over, religious faith is the wishful, willful denial that separation has occurred, that the caring maternal object, the ministering angel as it were, is gone, that ego boundaries differentiate the big one and the little one. What James ([1902] 1987) calls the faith-state arises unconsciously from precisely this early object-relation, which is deeply internalized into the perceptual system.

Again, the wondrous sense of God's presence, or the remarkable coincidence that one regards as a miracle (sometimes the synchronous result of supplication) is essentially the "return of the repressed," the wishful, unconscious resurgence of the period in which the original version of such events was the order of the day, the period during which the religious universe began to emerge from the powerful Winnicottian illusions. In this way, miracles of prayer are instances not of the supernatural but of the uncanny. It is as if the universe is still in the orbit of the believer's wish and will. What actually happened before appears to be happening again when it isn't "supposed to happen," when the caregiver and the child are separate from one another. Supernatural events and personages in the religious realm are the result of ego boundaries dissolving. Indeed, the religious realm as a whole is unconsciously designed to accomplish such a dissolution, and that is why we are obliged to view religion as regressive. It permits the psychic remerger of parent and child. The miracle of faith resides here. Not only does one get the caregiver back, but one gets the caregiver back in an idealized form. One is not alone, and one has nothing to fear from a just and merciful God. What joyful tidings! Or in modern psychological terms, what a formula for mitigating the stresses of human existence.

The Container of Space

Like time, space is closely associated with the first relationship. Indeed, psychic space comprises a kind of container which can be originally connected to the maternal caretaking function and to the absorption of infantile fantasies and fears. The capacity to experience space is a primary aspect of the ego, which seems to have emerged from sensations upon the fetal skin at birth, thereby awakening the skin, with its sense receptors, into its function as a surface, as a boundary between self and nonself, and as a container of the self. Without the development of such a psychic space there can be, quite simply, no perception (Grotstein 1978).

The baby's nonverbalized feelings often discover their expression through the skin: it may itch, weep, rage, and so forth. Such exigencies will be dealt with by the mother according to her ability to accept and soothe the blemished infant who will, in turn, internalize the experience. The mother demonstrates how the containing figure, herself, is experienced concretely as a skin. It is precisely this function that triggers the rudimentary idea of external and internal space (Pines 1980).

The defensive strategies of the early time are formed within levels of spatial representation which are the cognitive matrix out of which defensive strategies arise. When we withdraw, we withdraw to some place, some psychic place, that allows us to withdraw there. We split the maternal figure off to another place, which permits us to split it off. We reduce the world to a space in which we dwell securely, our substitute womb of enumerated types. The very notion of separateness implies exclusion and boundaries that establish the end of one individual and the beginning of another. When the French philosopher Gaston Bachelard (1969, 5) reminds us that "all really inhabited space bears the essence of the notion of home," he only calls to mind the connection between spatial representation and the problem of mothering, for all notions of home bear the essence of the notion of mother. Eventually we will see how all of this bears upon one of the Western world's most influential prayers, Psalm 23.

The Word

Nearly half a century ago, the pioneering investigations of the Russian linguist Vygotsky (1979) made clear that the development of language was not primarily a cognitive process (the orthodox view) but an interactive, social process loaded with emotional, bodily components from the preverbal period. Because thought and speech develop in a parallel and reciprocal fashion, we must ultimately think of language as a dynamic system of meaning in which the emotional and the intellectual unite. The egocentric speech of the three-year-old does not disappear when the child reaches seven or eight. Instead of atrophying, such egocentric speech goes underground, that is, it turns into inner speech and forms the foundation of that inward babble which, joined to higher cognitive components, comes eventually to comprise a sizeable portion of our ordinary consciousness. In this way, the development of thinking is not from the individual to the social but from the social to the individual. The child starts conversing with himself as he has been doing with others.

As for the spoken word, it is initially a substitute for the gesture, for the bodily attitude and bodily expression that precede the verbalized sound. When the child says "mama," it is not merely the word that means, say, put me in the chair, but the child's whole behavior at that moment, his reaching out for the chair, trying to hold it, etc. In contrast to the egocentric speech that goes inward, verbalized speech goes outward; the child uses it as a method of pointing. It is the fusion of this inward speech and developing outward speech that finally comprises human thought in its ordinary, basic expression.

We appreciate from this viewpoint the growing psychological realization, based explicitly on Vygotsky's work, that thinking is an unconscious process in the first instance (Basch 1981). Even our conscious speech, the psychological community has come to recognize, is pervaded by unconscious mechanisms to the degree that it is tied to our thinking (Roustang 1976). This means that our thinking, our stream of consciousness itself in the most general, all-inclusive sense, is the source of those slips of the tongue on which Freud stumbled nearly a century ago.

With regard to the role of separation in all of this, we must note that symbol formation (or word formation) arises from the infant's shared experience with the mother (Bleich 1990). The common act of referential pointing starts with the mother's invitation but soon leads to the child inviting the mother to join in the contemplation of some object. This marks the beginning of what psychologists call intellectual stereoscopy, in which the objectification of the world is dependent on social interaction. The child names things to someone, and the loving feedback he receives becomes the incentive for naming further things. The whole idea of two-ness and separateness arises from this mutuality. Thus the presence and absence of the mother and of important physical objects in the child's world play motivational roles in the development of representational thought.

In fact, the ability to recognize mother, to conceptualize her as mother, is goaded into existence by the need to cope with her absence, or loss. The feeling of loss becomes the motive for "acquiring the capacity to represent absent objects or to represent objects regardless of their presence or absence." When the baby names the absent object, he predicates it on the basis of its former presence: thus, mommy gone. The same act can predicate a future presence on a current absence. The ideas of gone and mommy are linked and placed in relation to one another (Bleich 1990). The whole business of linguistic predication is thus associated with the problem of separation from the caretaker. Again, as the child links up mommy and gone, he creates a dependent relationship between two ideas that substitutes for each idea's dependency on actual experience. This gives the child the power to recall the mother at will. Symbolic representation (as we saw in Winnicott's discussion of play) comes to comprise a way back to the missing object of one's emotions.

Because the verbal representation of the thing is the culmination of the symbolic process, the word is the magical tie that reunites us with the all-important figure(s) of infancy and childhood. It is not merely that maternal stimulation during the time of language development is necessary for the fulfillment of the child's potential; our symbolic seeing is charged with the emotional energy that went into our life and death struggle to maintain our connection to the caregiver at the same time we were giving her up. Through the early imperfections of mothering, we learn to grip the world with our bodies, with our tense anticipation (the time sense). Through the crises of separation, which continue to transpire after the early period, we learn to grip the world with our minds, with our symbols, with our words. The mirror phase of infancy eventually gives way to the presentational mirror of a mind that has separation on its mind. The very running on of our thoughts in ordinary consciousness becomes a link to the figures of the past. To express the matter in terms that recall the context of our discussion explicitly, because the word becomes the child's chief tool for "matching mental states" (Plotkin 1997, 249), the word also becomes the

child's chief tool for preserving the attunement and evoked companionship from which Winnicottian illusions arise. Thus language as the substance of prayer, or as the attempt to dissolve the ego boundary which
differentiates caregiver and child, harbors perforce the unconscious aims
and wishes of the early period as they inform the supplications of the adult.
In the universe of religious behavior, the word always reaches back to its
primitive communicative origins.

The Oedipus, and After

Internalization of stress does not cease with the close of the primary
years. On the contrary, the newcomer emerges from this turbulent period to
confront the strain of the Oedipal phase during which the emotional and
sensual desire for the parent of the opposite sex creates a fear of castration
in the male child (we will come to the female in a moment), as well as powerful feelings of ambivalence and jealousy toward the male parent.

This is a time of great anxiety for the boy, whose dilemma will be imper-
fectly and paradoxically resolved through identification with the father.
That is to say, perceiving the hopelessness of removing his rival, the child
begins to identify with him (identification is a form of internalization) and
to strive and compete in the male world of which the father is the chief representative. As his wounded narcissism benefits from his boyish accomplishments and interactions, he gradually adopts the male point of view.
Typically, his wishes and aims are now bound up with heroic achievements, glory, domination; yet the wish for the mother persists at the deepest levels, and a conflicted dependency on the father develops as a refuge
from separation and loss.

The entire syndrome—to use the presently popular term—finds its expression in romantic and/or authoritarian fantasies and behaviors. As
males, we go through life longing for the perfect woman (which means the
mother), fearing emasculation at the hands of both women and men, iden-
tifying with symbols of power and control (the nation, the leader, the company, the winning team, wealth), and making the best of what we perceive
to be our failures and shortcomings. It is a pathetic picture and would even
be ridiculous were it not so replete with deep and genuine discontentment.
When thousands of years ago, the Buddha bluntly maintained that life is
suffering, he probably had some ancient version of this syndrome in mind.

For the female child, the dynamics of the Oedipal phase are rather different; the stress that results, however, can be just as intense. If a single utterance had to be made to get at the essentials of the matter, it would point out
that the girl's partial absorption (as opposed to the boy's almost total ab-

sorption) into the father's socially oriented universe during the resolution of the Oedipal crisis leaves the female child more directly and uninterruptedly in the midst of the pre-Oedipal, maternally centered issues that characterize the first years of life. Hence the girl is more prone than the boy to evince open, ongoing concern with boundary issues, or issues of separation and merger, and to regard the male parent (and his later substitutes) not so much as an avenue away from the mother's world as a means of resolving problems inextricably tied to the imperfections of the mother's care (see Gilligan 1982).

In even briefer compass, girls (and women) remain absorbed in the issue of closeness, and when girls (and women) discover themselves involved with normal males who fear such closeness, whose pursuits have been directed away from precisely such closeness, the old, familiar tension between the sexes results. Women tend to experience confusion when the needs of the self, particularly the assertive, aggressive self, clash with the need to preserve and enhance relationships, to express care and concern. Men, placing the emphasis on separation and achievement, typically experience less confusion as the needs of the self arise during periods of interpersonal and professional crisis, but they may also harbor an underlying sense of isolation, a loneliness and disconnectedness that often plagues them throughout the course of their lives (see Flax 1990).

Several years after the close of the Oedipal period adolescence brings forth its weighty issues: genital sexuality, increasing separation from the parental presence, the forging of a consistent, integrated character, and a growing awareness of adult imperfections. It is a formidable list, and for millions, a hellish time, exacerbated today by a decline of familial support and cohesion, by a world of impersonal technological forces and influences, by an increasingly unhealthful, polluted environment (adult failure at the stewardship of the planet), and by the annihilative, "doomsday" weaponry of several "sovereign nations." Of course neither Oedipal nor adolescent issues are strictly perceptual ones, as the issues of the mirror and separation stages are. By the age of six, and obviously by the age of twelve or thirteen, the perceptual apparatus in its underlying, unconscious essentials is complete. Indeed, the Oedipal period and adolescence characteristically inherit, and are shaped by, the problems and forces of the foundational years (see Dorpat 1988). And that is the point. The stress of the later dilemmas deepens the primal, mind-body anxiety that we have been describing in the context. Our projective style of perceiving the world is considerably intensified as Oedipal and adolescent conflicts absorb the struggles of the early time.

Qualifications and Reaffirmations: A Final Preparatory Word

The question arises: Does the generalized model that I have presented thus far apply to all children, in all families, in all cultures, in our rapidly changing world? No one will deny that children, mothers, fathers, and families vary considerably in regard to developmental tendencies and interrelational styles. Mahler herself is careful to point out again and again that quality of response and rate of maturation differ dramatically among her youthful subjects and that such difference is compounded by the uniqueness of each parent and each familial situation. Mary Ainsworth (1983) and her associates have confirmed that babies do not react uniformly to specifically the problem of physical separation. For some, the departure or the absence of the caretaker is far more traumatic than it is for others. As for reunion, some children are reluctant to "make up" for a lengthy period; others are happily in their parent's arms right away. Yet the separation-union conflict is there to one degree or another in all children, all parents, and all families. We know babyhood and symbiosis at the beginning; later, we know individuation and relative autonomy. As Anette Karmiloff-Smith (1995, 206) expresses it in her excellent book, *Baby It's You*, "attachment to mother—and anxiety at being separated from her—appear to be phenomena that occur in all cultures of the world. They are what we know as developmental universals, like grasping, babbling, and other such behaviors. Studies have identified attachment and anxiety in children of roughly the same age in cultures as diverse as America, Botswana, Israel, and Guatemala." Mahler's phases, and the issues that pertain to them, appear to be ubiquitous.

Accordingly, when we apply the model in the present case, we will find that certain points are particularly relevant to certain prayers and rituals, and that other points pertain especially to other supplications and rites. We will discover that some believers are more susceptible to problems of separation and union than other believers are. The psychoanalytic approach will be very significant here and not very significant there. Some aspects of faith may escape us altogether. The point is, our model will be strong enough to tell us a great deal about prayer and that is all we can expect from it. To demand absolute relevance and certainty in regard to each and every prayer would be perverse. The inexact human sciences simply do not work that way. In the end, we do the best we can with the data that we have, and we leave it to those who come later to improve upon our findings. This is called the dialectical method.

Similar reflections may be brought to bear when Peter Neubauer (1985) informs us that the mother is not always the central presence during the early period, that our rapidly changing culture increasingly witnesses the father (and others) assuming a pivotal role. Undoubtedly this is so. But even here, where fathers or uncles or nannies or aunts are conspicuous, the issue of separation-union will still be crucial for the developing child. Motivational dynamics may shift direction, yet the scheme that Mahler gives us will continue to disclose essential conflicts and provide a useful foundation. I am not denying that future decades may require wholesale reformulation; I am only suggesting that we should continue to make theories, based on our best evidence, while the world around us continues to change. What choice have we, after all? Were we to wait for change to stop so that we could begin to make theories, we would never make any theories.

With regard to cross-cultural issues, which we can only apprehend as formidable, we must remember, first, that we are dealing here with primarily Western materials; hence our analyses will jibe reasonably well with Mahler's developmental scheme, along with the expansion of it that we have undertaken in this chapter. Second, psychoanalytic studies of maturational problems among non-Western peoples reveal, on the one hand, the enormous differences at work in the world, and on the other, the ubiquity of the separation-union conflict.

East Indians, for example, struggle mightily to achieve a coherent, separate self amidst a consuming and often maddening network of familial ties and responsibilities (see Kakar 1995). The Japanese struggle similarly with the powerful demands of the work group, a conformist, authoritarian extension of the original family structure (see Roland 1988). And the struggles of both these peoples are complicated and deepened by the arrival of Western, often American, ideas and attitudes. Yet for all the differences, which I do not for one minute propose to minimize, we still see the basic, core conflict over union and separation as it emerges from Mahler and as it may be cautiously extrapolated to the adolescents and adults of other societies. Indeed, this primal struggle exists worldwide and is perhaps best illustrated in Eli Sagan's (1985) monumental study of various cultures—each of which appears to be negotiating a stage of Mahler's scheme.

Maintaining that "the psyche is the paradigm for the development of culture and society," and following closely Mahler's depiction of psychic development, Sagan views the human community as a whole passing from (a) early kinship organizations rooted in the familial bond, to (b) complex organizations based on chiefs and kings and comprising the first, wrenching move away from kinship, to (c) archaic civilizations (Egypt, China) based on the elaborate, hierarchical arrangements that ensure individual security through stable social order. Sagan writes,

> Society may choose to resist . . . the drive toward development, but
> once advance is resolved upon, society is not free to take any direction
> . . . it wants. No primitive society develops into an archaic or classical
> civilization. Every primitive society that embarks on a developmen-
> tal journey becomes a complex society. The logic within this advance
> is not primarily economic, or scientific, or even rational; . . . it is pri-
> marily a psychological logic. The stages in development from primi-
> tive to chieftainship to early monarchies to complex monarchies to
> archaic civilizations are projections and magnifications onto society
> as a whole of stages in the development of the psyche. The journey of
> the psyche through the various phases in the process of separation
> and individuation is recapitulated in social development. (364)

As for the advanced, democratic society in which we exist today, it is "the
least dependent upon fundamental kinship ties of any political system ever
invented" (375). For Sagan, then, the developmental conflict described by
Mahler is not only ubiquitous for the individual but for the group as well;
the world struggles with problems of merger and separation, with the
clashing needs for cohesion and personal, independent expression. With all
of this in mind, let us turn to prayer and faith.

NOTES

1. Suzanne Kirschner explores this issue at length in her volume *The Religious
and Romantic Origins of Psychoanalysis* (1996). Kirschner writes (1996, 13):

> In contemporary society, many of us look to psychoanalysis to tell us the truth
> about ourselves. Even with the current ascendance of biological models in
> psychiatry, both Freudian and post-Freudian approaches remain powerfully
> attractive to many clinicians, scholars, and laypersons; they continue to exert
> a strong hold on our cultural and scientific imaginations. What accounts for
> these theories' resonance and appeal? In this book I suggest that much of the
> compelling quality of contemporary psychoanalysis derives from the fact
> that it is deeply rooted in Western religious and cultural values.

A psychoanalytic account of development may be a secularized version of the biblical fall of man and man's ultimate redemption. Accordingly, those who create
"theories of human development" must be careful to hold in check their own "ideals of personhood" (Kirschner 1996, 13) as they conduct their research and an-
nounce their conclusions, while those of us who read and evaluate such theories
must keep a sharp eye out for unwarranted assumptions and slanted, emotional
interpretations. Obviously Kirschner's book is not going to make analytic models
of development disappear; as I maintained in chapter 1 and will continue to maintain here, we cannot understand our behavior as grownups without also under-

standing our development as children. Moreover, a fully secularized psychoanalytic account of our human experience from start to finish is so qualitatively different from its spiritual forebears as to make Kirschner's tight parallels suspect. It is not psychoanalysis that reflects religious myth and romanticism; it is romanticism and religious myth that reflect the "tragedy" of human development (separation from the parent) and its wishful, projective resolution in God or in nature (regaining the parent). Psychoanalysis finally brings all this to consciousness. Kirschner may have it backwards. Still, her book does alert us to the hazards of the enterprise, and we might keep it in mind as we proceed.

2. Not surprisingly, various features of Mahler's developmental model have been challenged since its inception twenty-five years ago. Feminist Jane Flax (1990), for example, suggests that Mahler in several places is not sufficiently sensitive to gender differences. All things considered, however, Mahler's scheme remains not only the best one available to us, but a major contribution to our understanding of human behavior—in Western culture anyway. See also Kirschner (1996) on this score.

3. Mahler's postulation of a normal autistic phase in which the infant experiences and internalizes symbiotic merger with the mothering figure, and in particular Mahler's suggestion that we as adults can regress to this autism, and know it regressively, has stirred controversy. G.E. Zuriff (1992) has synthesized and summarized the literature, and I refer the reader to his paper cited in the reference section. Incidentally, Zuriff finds nothing objectionable in Mahler's postulation of primary autism, remarking (30) that it is not strictly speaking "empirical" yet retains its "scientific status" as a "theoretical postulate."

REFERENCES

Ainsworth, M. 1983. "Patterns of Infant-Mother Attachment." In *Human Development*, ed. D. Magnusson and V. Allen. New York: Academic Press.

Bachelard, G. 1969. *The Poetics of Space*. Trans. M. Jolas. Boston: Beacon Press.

Basch, M. 1981. "Psychoanalytic Interpretation and Cognitive Transformation." *International Journal of Psychoanalysis* 62: 151–74.

Bleich, D. 1990. *New Considerations of the Infantile Acquisition of Language and Symbolic Thought*. Presented to Psychological Center for the Study of the Arts. State University of New York, Buffalo, 1990, 1–28

Blum, H. 1994 "The Conceptual Development of Regression." *The Psychoanalytic Study of the Child* 49: 60–76.

Bollas, C. 1987. *The Shadow of the Object: Psychoanalysis of the Unthought-Known*. London: Free Association Books.

Delgado, J. 1971. *Physical Control of the Mind*. New York: Harper and Row.

De Mause, L. 1982. *Foundations of Psychohistory*. New York: Creative Roots.

Dorpat, T. 1988. "Man and Mind: Collected Papers of Jeanne Lampel-De Groot." *Seattle Institute for Psychoanalysis Newsletter* 2: 4–5.

Eigen, M. 1985. "Toward Bion's Starting Point." *International Journal of Psychoanalysis* 66: 321–30.

Flax, J. 1990. *Thinking Fragments: Psychoanalysis, Feminism, and Postmodernism in the Contemporary West*. Berkeley: University of California Press.

Freud, S. [1930] 1961. *Civilization and Its Discontents*. Trans. J. Strachey. New York: Norton.

Gallagher, W. 1992. "Motherless Child." *The Sciences*, July, 12–15.

Gilligan, C. 1982. *In a Different Voice*. Cambridge: Harvard University Press.

Grotstein, J. 1978. "Inner Space: Its Dimensions and Coordinates." *International Journal of Psychoanalysis* 59: 53–61.

Hale, N., Jr. 1995. *The Rise and Crisis of Psychoanalysis in the United States*. Vol. 2. New York: Oxford University Press.

Hartocollis, P. 1974. "Origins of Time." *Psychoanalytic Quarterly* 43: 243–61.

Horgan, J. 1996. "Why Freud Isn't Dead." *Scientific American*, December, 106–11.

James, W. [1902] 1987. *The Varieties of Religious Experience*. New York: Library of America.

Kakar, S. 1995. "Clinical Work and Cultural Imagination." *Psychoanalytic Quarterly* 64: 265–81.

Karmiloff-Smith, A. 1995. *Baby It's You*. London: Ebury Press.

Kirschner, S. 1996. *The Religious and Romantic Origins of Psychoanalysis: Individuation and Integration in Post-Freudian Theory*. Cambridge: Cambridge University Press.

Levy, D. 1996. *Freud among the Philosophers: The Psychoanalytic Unconscious and Its Philosophical Critics*. New Haven: Yale University Press.

Liechty, D. 1999. "Freud and the Question of Pseudoscience." *The Ernest Becker Foundation Newsletter* 6: 6–7.

Mahler, M. 1968. *On Human Symbiosis and the Vicissitudes of Individuation*. New York: International Universities Press.

Mahler, M., F. Pine, and A. Bergman. 1975. *The Psychological Birth of the Human Infant*. New York: Basic Books.

Meissner, W. 1984. *Psychoanalysis and Religious Experience*. New Haven: Yale University Press.

Neubauer, P. 1985. "Preoedipal Objects and Object Primacy." *Psychoanalytic Study of the Child* 40: 163–82.

Neumann, E. 1970. *The Great Mother*. Trans. R. Manheim. Princeton: Princeton University Press.

Parker, R. 1995. *Mother Love/Mother Hate*. New York: Basic Books.

Person, E. 1990. *Dreams of Love and Fateful Encounters*. London: Penguin Books.

Pines, D. 1980. "Skin Communication." *International Journal of Psychoanalysis* 61: 315–24.

Plotkin, H. 1997. *Evolution in Mind: An Introduction to Evolutionary Psychology*. London: Penguin Books.

Rheingold, J. 1964. *The Fear of Being a Woman*. New York: Grune and Stratton.

Rizzuto, A.-M. 1979. *The Birth of the Living God: A Psychoanalytic Study*. Chicago: University of Chicago Press.

Rogers, R. 1991. *Self and Other: Object Relations in Psychoanalysis and Literature*. New York: New York University Press.

Roland, A. 1988. *In Search of Self in India and Japan*. Princeton: Princeton University Press.

Roustang, F. 1976. *Dire Mastery: Discipleship from Freud to Lacan*. Trans. N. Lukacher. Baltimore: Johns Hopkins University Press.

Sagan, E. 1985. *At the Dawn of Tyranny*. New York: Knopf.

Shaw, M. 1995. *Your Anxious Child*. New York: Birch Lane Press.

Southwood, H. 1973. "The Origin of Self Awareness and Ego Behavior." *International Journal of Psychoanalysis* 54: 235–39.

Spitz, R. 1965. *The First Year of Life*. New York: International Universities Press.

Steinzor, B. 1979. "Death and the Construction of Reality." *Omega: Journal of Death and Dying* 9: 97–124.

Stern, D. 1985. *The Interpersonal World of the Infant*. New York: Basic Books.

Vygotsky, L. [1934] 1979. *Thought and Language*. Trans. E. Hanfmann and G. Vakar. Cambridge: MIT Press.

Webster, R. 1995. *Why Freud Was Wrong: Sin, Science, and Psychoanalysis*. New York: Basic Books.

Winnicott, D. 1971. *Playing and Reality*. London: Penguin.

Zuriff, G. 1992. "Theoretical Inference and the New Psychoanalytic Theories of Infancy." *Psychoanalytic Quarterly* 61: 18–35.

CHAPTER 3

MAGIC, FAITH, AND PRAYER

THE FOCUS OF THINGS TO COME

Personal, individual, informal prayer, as opposed to codified, congregational prayer, is my main interest, although I will touch upon congregational supplication in one or two places. This opposition, as it turns out, has a complex, disputatious history, which is not our business here. It is enough to say that the individualism of prayer is usually traced back to Jeremiah and the psalms of the Old Testament, that Jesus' prayer on the Mount is widely regarded as the model prayer for individual Christians ("Not my will but Thine be done") (see Heiler [1932] 1997, 123), that Paul views personal, intercessory prayer as a cornerstone of spiritual practice, and that by Luther's day subjective, solitary prayer in which the worshipper gives himself over to a fervent, one-to-One relationship with his God, is moving steadily toward the heart of Christianity, first for the Protestant and then, with rather less momentum perhaps, for the Catholic as well. For both Jews (see Jacobs 1995, 380) and Muslims (see Heiler [1932] 1997, 123), codified, public prayer is the dominant form of worship, although there are noteworthy exceptions—chiefly in the area of mysticism. Accordingly then, and in the most general, preliminary way, what follows will find us exploring from a psychological angle the motivational dynamics of personal prayer in the Judeo-Christian tradition.

This tradition contains at its core (mysticism for the moment aside) an essentially anthropomorphic, supernatural Deity capable of receiving, understanding, and responding to the personal, private, subjective, spoken, and unspoken prayers of individual religious practitioners. He hears and He answers (or chooses not to answer). "All religion," writes Karen Armstrong in *A History of God* (1993, 48), "must begin with some anthropomorphism." I will be dealing in what follows only with such a Deity and only with prayers directed to such a Deity. Conversely, I will not be dealing here with any form of secularized prayer, with prayer as a method of "getting in touch with one's feelings," or "looking inwardly" for one's "innermost self," with prayer as a "breathless response" to a "magnificent sunset," or a "bird on the wing." Mind you, I have nothing against this sort of thing. I consider myself as spiritual as the next person. I'm just not dealing with it in chapter 3 of this book. God's anthropomorphism, and in particular the way in which that anthropomorphism is treated in the literature of prayer, resides at the very center of my overall presentation. Let the reader prepare himself, then, for what he can think of generally as good old-fashioned prayer emanating from good old-fashioned pray-ers.

I will rely on a wide variety of sources, from the outcries of medieval saints to the musings of New Age gurus, from the reflections of present-day preachers to the remarks of neoclassical philosophers. From the lush, endless garden of prayer I will pluck what I need. However, for much of the discussion I will utilize three pivotal, relatively recent treatments of the subject, namely Friedrich Heiler's *Prayer* ([1932] 1997), regarded by Hans Küng as the classical work on the topic and perhaps the most scholarly and comprehensive book on prayer ever to appear in the West; Ole Hallesby's *Prayer* ([1948] 1979), another classic, translated into several languages, reprinted fifteen times in English alone, and probably the most widely read and influential single discussion composed during the twentieth century; Romano Guardini's *Prayer in Practice* (1957), a treasured work among Roman Catholics and penned by one of the Church's most astute and respected thinkers—undoubtedly another classic treatment.[1] I will also turn in a number of places to James's incomparable *The Varieties of Religious Experience* ([1902] 1987), a volume that has served me well to this point. Needless to say, for all these authors, prayer and faith are inextricably intertwined: faith depends on prayer for its existence, and prayer is nothing other than faith's signal manifestation. "We must bear in mind," declares Guardini (1957, 209), "that faith itself depends on prayer. . . . Prayer is the basic act of faith as breathing is the basic act of life." Until we pray, maintains Hallesby ([1948] 1979, 24), we have no access to God, and God has no access to us. He "cannot gain admittance." To pray is to believe. Faith is "prayer and nothing but prayer," writes Heiler ([1932] 1997, xiii), echoing Martin Luther. Without prayer we "cannot find God." Prayer, contends

James ([1902] 1987, 416), "is the very soul and essence of religion." Where prayer is lacking, "there is no religion." Thus the basic question arises, how does one go about this praying? What is required of the worshipper to demonstrate his faith effectively through prayer, to successfully contact the Deity, to move into the supernatural sphere—in a word, to be religious?

Helplessness and Dependency

One must, first of all, adopt a certain attitude, a certain psychological posture, or stance. One does not come to God in just any way, but in a very specific way indeed. I'm referring to an attitude of utter dependency, utter helplessness, utter submission, a willful attempt to get rid of one's will entirely. "Helplessness," writes Hallesby ([1948] 1979, 13), "is unquestionably the first and surest indication of a praying heart. As far as I can see, prayer has been ordained only for the helpless." Hallesby goes on in the personal style that has made his book so influential: "listen, my friend! Your helplessness is your best prayer. It calls from your heart to the heart of God with greater effect than all your uttered pleas. He hears it from the very moment that you are seized with helplessness, and He becomes actively engaged at once in hearing and answering the prayer of your helplessness" (14). Thus "helplessness is the real secret and impelling power of prayer" (17), the "very essence of prayer" (16), the "decisive factor" that makes us "attached to God" and "more strongly dependent on Him" (21). At the heart of successful prayer, states Heiler ([1932] 1997, 258), dwells the "expression" of one's "weakness and dependency." One "submits" entirely to "God's will" and strives to make such "submission" a "permanent attitude" (268). In fact, the "feeling of dependence" is the "universal feeling" that "animates" the whole of humanity's relations with the Deity; "nowhere . . . is it revealed so clearly as in prayer" (77). "Man is ever conscious of his want and helplessness," maintains Guardini (1957, 78); "it is only right, therefore, that he should turn to the bountiful and almighty God, who is not only ready to give and to help, but greatly rejoices in it." Unless we "surrender without reservation" to the "Creator," Guardini continues (1957, 64), unless we realize that our very existence depends upon God and His grace, our praying will be futile. While our powers are limited, even puny, God's are infinite. He allows us to breathe, to be, and above all to approach Him with "our needs" (134). Identical views may be instantly discovered in a thousand places. Dependence upon and submission to the Almighty reside at the very core of Judaism (see Crim 1989, 385), and of Islam as well (see Hinnells 1991, 152). "Thy will be done," writes Cotter in *How To Pray* (1999, 28). The "value of surrender" in prayer is "extraordinary," declares Dossey in

Healing Words (1993, 100–101). "Asking is our staple diet," asserts Lindsay in *Prayer That Moves Mountains* (1996, 37), and he goes on: "God's plan involves daily dependence on Him. Without Him we can do nothing." Nor is it only one's inward attitude, or stance, that determines the emotional, psychological quality of one's praying. One's bodily conduct may also enter integrally into the picture. One can, of course, worship in any manner one chooses, at any time, in any place, in any posture. Yet for countless millions everywhere, inward dependency, helplessness, and submission are outwardly expressed, or mirrored, by prayer's traditional, ritualistic behaviors: suppliants kneel, bow down, close their eyes, fold their hands, even prostrate themselves entirely. Stephen Winward, in *Teach Yourself How to Pray* (1961, 46), cites Psalm 95 as follows: "O come, let us worship and bow down, let us kneel before the Lord." In these "familiar words of the Venite," he observes, "the Psalmist invites us to let our bodies also participate in the worship of God." Let's take a moment now to see how this theme of dependency, of helplessness, of submission is developed in the literature we are employing.

"If you are a mother," asserts Hallesby ([1948] 1979, 14), "you will understand very readily this aspect of prayer. Your infant child cannot formulate in words a single petition to you. Yet the little one prays the best way he knows how. All he can do is cry, but you understand very well his pleading cry. Moreover, the little one need not even cry. All you need to do is to see him in all his helpless dependence upon you, and a prayer touches your mother-heart, a prayer which is stronger than the loudest cry. He who is Father of all that is called mother and all that is called child in heaven and on earth deals with us in the same way." Thus we leave everything "in His hands" (105). We cling in our helplessness to the "spirit of prayer" whenever we pray (102). We know "the Lord is at our side," and therefore we no longer feel frightened (119). Indeed, we know He is there constantly, and so we may tell Him "throughout the day," and during the nighttime too, "how dependent we are upon Him" (121). When his own "little boy" comes to him with "round baby eyes" and asks for his assistance, Hallesby writes (121), he sees at once the manner in which everyone should approach the "heavenly Father" (121).

And by the way, Hallesby is perfectly aware of the psychological dimension of the discussion; he is not using the theme of dependency in some metaphorical fashion: "psychologically," he states (25), "helplessness is the sustaining and impelling power of prayer." Heiler ([1932] 1997, 32) agrees and also turns to childhood in illustration. The feeling of "dependence and impotence" is the key to successful praying, for we have no genuine power of our own: we are like "children who can do nothing" (36). It is precisely this childlike mindset, this childlike "trust and surrender," holds Heiler (130–31), that marks all the "eminent men" with "a genius for prayer," all the "great men of religion" (253). We turn to God "in prayer," writes Guardini (1957, 77), "as the child in distress turns to his mother." Jesus taught us, Guardini goes on (77), "that we should turn to the Father and ask Him" for our "daily bread," for the "necessities" of our "daily life." This is because the Almighty knows best what is needful for us. He knows how to love us truly, how to look after us in every respect—in a word, how to care for us in our helplessness and want (78). To pray successfully, then, one must return, or perhaps regress, to an earlier stage of one's psychosexual development, to a period during which helplessness, weakness, and dependency were the chief characteristics of one's interactions with other people. One must somehow discover again the infantile, childlike attitudes that overrode one's inchoate personality during life's preliminary stages. Indeed, unless one does this, unless one blurs ego boundaries and attaches oneself dependently to God, one has no hope of succeeding. One's helplessness is one's principal agent. Thus a further question arises.

Why does successful prayer hinge so decisively upon the assumption of an infantile, childlike state, a state of dependence, helplessness, and submission? To respond, I must recall the opening sentence of my overall summary, proffered in chapter 1: "individual, subjective prayer, the kind we discover in James, is finally an instance of homeopathic magical conduct." It enacts magically, or renders magically, something other than itself, something that lies behind it, or beneath it, something that serves as its emotional, psychological antecedent, its natural, behavioral wellspring, or source—in a very real sense, its inspiration. The famous Jungian scholar, Erich Neumann, provides us with a hint in his celebrated volume, *The Great Mother* (1970, 115), when he writes, "the original magical intention to move and influence the upper powers is preserved in almost all prayer." To reveal the magical quality of prayer rigorously, however, we must investigate magic's essential nature, its ubiquitous role in human affairs, and we must do so in the light of our contextual psychoanalytic discussions. If we can wed our psychology to an anthropological-philosophical grasp of magical conduct we just might engender the kind of understanding that will lead us (naturalistically, of course) to the nucleus of prayer, and to the nucleus of prayer's mysterious parent-offspring, religious faith. We might come to realize that the powers which supplicatory magic strives to influence are powers whose origin lies very close to home.

TOWARD THE MAGIC OF PRAYER

Anthropological attempts to fathom magical behavior commenced in earnest during the course of the nineteenth century and culminated in Sir James Frazer's monumental study, *The Golden Bough*, originally published in England in 1890. The century as a whole was given to what we may regard as an "us and them" approach to things, an approach that crept unhindered into many fields of intellectual endeavor, including anthropology and comparative religion. Over here were enlightened, contemporary, Christianized Europeans of good social and economic standing, and over there were pagans and primitives past and present, prone to quaint, crude, formulaic attempts at controlling a world they didn't understand scientifically (an exception was sometimes made for the ancient Hebrews, one of whom was, after all, Jesus Christ). Primitive magic was goal directed (or "efficacious") superstition; it was tied to power-charged objects and spells wielded by all manner of purblind necromancers, from exotic tribal chiefs to lowly, credulous villagers mumbling over navel-strings and afterbirths. Frazer's towering book, which still repays investigation, harbored in its core a loyalty to the progressive or perhaps evolutional notions of the day: humankind was culturally, intellectually, spiritually on the move, from the stage of primitive magic to the stage of religion (a refinement of primitive magic), to the stage of rational, scientific understanding which for some of Frazer's contemporaries was compatible with refined religion (the old Baconian ideal of the New Atlantis) and which for others (say, Freud and his circle) was not.

Although Frazer's progressive vision was historically and culturally problematical, to put it mildly, it became (and remains) widely popular in England, on the Continent, and in North America. Yet that vision also nourished fierce controversies over the nature of enlightened religion, controversies which proved useful to those who took up magic and religion during the course of the twentieth century. For example, the famous Scottish historian-anthropologist, Robertson Smith (1842–96), one of Frazer's intellectual mentors, opined that certain denominations, such as Catholicism, were more reluctant than other denominations, such as Protestantism, to jettison their magical baggage and join the parade toward refinement. Further, he was inclined to express this view in his well-attended university lectures. "He could show with unrivalled erudition," writes Mary Douglas (1984, 18), that in the course of history "the ideals of Christianity . . . had moved from Catholic to Protestant forms." Needless to say, such scholarly conclusions might easily lead not only to bitter, partisan debate but to genuine confusion as to what exactly religion is, as distinguished from its putative forerunner, primitive magic. As I just suggested, twentieth-century anthropologists took the hint.

Although comparative studies of magic and religion are still disputatious, and will no doubt always be so given the deeply personal nature of religious belief, a general (as opposed to universal) consensus currently exists: religion and magic are closely affined, even connected inextricably, and it is more helpful, more productive of truth, to collapse the old dichotomy (including its "us-them" component) than to shore it up. Writes Mary Douglas in *Natural Symbols* ([1970] 1996, 7): "sacraments are one thing, magic another; taboos are one thing, sin another. The first thing is to break through the spiky verbal hedges that arbitrarily insulate one set of human experiences (ours) from another set (theirs)." She continues (9): "sacramental efficacy works internally; magical efficacy works externally. But this difference, even at the theological level, is less great than it seems. For if the theologian remembers to take account of the doctrine of the Incarnation, magical enough in itself, and the even more magical doctrine of the Resurrection and of how its power is channeled through the sacraments, he cannot make such a tidy distinction between sacramental and magical efficacy. Then there is the popular magicality in Christianity. A candle lit to St. Antony for finding a lost object is magical, as is also a St. Christopher medal used to prevent accidents . . . Both sacramental and magical behavior are expressions of ritualism." And finally, "I see no advantage . . . in making any distinction between magical and sacramental" (8).

Douglas renders the matter even more succinctly perhaps in her *Purity and Danger* (1984, 28): "the division between religion and magic" is "ill-considered." Indeed, "the more intractable puzzles in comparative religion arise because human experience has been thus wrongly divided." Such passages not only go to the heart of the matter, they allow us to witness firsthand the kind of professional insight that has prompted the *HarperCollins Dictionary of Religion* (see Smith 1995, 673) to present magic and religion as ultimately "compatible" for "twentieth-century scholars"; or the *Penguin Dictionary of Religions* (see Hinnells 1995, 282) to declare that "magic shades off into religion"; or the *Oxford Dictionary of World Religions* (see Bowker 1997, 598) to assert that for present-day anthropologists magic is "embedded in religion" where it "acts as an organization of context and meaning"; or the *Merriam-Webster's Encyclopedia of World Religions* (see Doniger 1999, 678) to view the notion that magic and religion are integrally related as a twentieth-century commonplace. Here are John and David Noss summing things up for us temperately in *A History of the World's Religions* (1990, 14, emphasis added): "magic may be loosely defined as an endeavor through utterance of set words, or the performance of set acts, or both, to control or bend the powers of the world to one's will. *It cannot be wholly divorced from religion,* . . . but it is discernibly present when the emphasis is placed on forcing things to happen rather than asking that they do."[2] Does this imply that magic may be covertly present in prayer, where the emphasis is placed on asking rather than forcing? I believe that it does, as I will soon try to establish. As for the us-them thinking that characterized Victorian approaches to magic and religion, it has bequeathed to us, once again in Mary Douglas's words (1984, 58), "a false distinction between primitive and modern cultures." It is a "mistake to suppose that there can be religion which is all interior, with no rules, no liturgy, no external signs of inward states. As with society, so with religion, external form is the condition of its existence" (62).

The proper model for appreciating "primitive ritual," observes Douglas (72), is not "the absurd Ali Baba" but the "figure of Freud." It is psychoanalysis precisely that can provide us with "pertinent suggestions" for the understanding of "religious beliefs" (72). Surely the great French anthropologist Marcel Mauss was thinking along similar lines when, several decades before the appearance of Professor Douglas's writings, he declared in *A General Theory of Magic* ([1903] 1972, 116), "in magic, as in religion, it is the unconscious ideas that are the active ones." Accordingly, the old us-them dichotomy must be retired from active service lest it wreak still more havoc on our comprehension of human behavior. Let's give Susanne Langer (1988, 307) the last word on the subject: "once we recognize a truly primitive trait of human experience in a naïve form, we usually end up by finding it still operative in our own subjective experience." We have far too much history behind us as millennial Westerners to doubt the veracity of that sentence.

Frazer provides us with a useful, preliminary framework in *The Golden Bough* ([1990] 1959, 35): "magic rests everywhere," he remarks, "on two fundamental principles: first, that *like produces like,* effect resembling cause; second, that *things which have once been in contact continue ever afterwards to act on each other.*" The "former principle" is tied to homeopathic or imitative magic, the "latter" to the contagious variety. Let's open with contagion, "the most familiar example" of which is the "magical sympathy" that is "supposed to exist between a man and any severed portion of his person, such as his hair or nails; so that whoever gets possession of human hair or nails may work his will, at any distance, upon the person from whom they were cut" (62). Frazer goes on: "other parts which are commonly believed to remain in a sympathetic union with the body, after the physical connexion has been severed, are the navel-string and the afterbirth, including the placenta. So intimate, indeed, is the union conceived to be, that the

fortunes of the individual for good or evil throughout life are often supposed to be bound up with one or other of these portions of his person, so
that if his navel-string or afterbirth is preserved and properly treated, he
will be prosperous; whereas if it be injured or lost, he will suffer accordingly" (63). Again, "magic may be wrought on a man sympathetically not
only through his clothes and severed parts of himself, but also through
the impressions left by his body in sand or earth. In particular, it is a
worldwide superstition that by injuring footprints you injure the feet that
made them" (68).

We may think of contagion generally as a transfer of power by contact or
by proximity, and as a species of magic that is frequently associated with sacred objects and with pollution (see Smith 1995, 287). In illustration of homeopathic or imitative magic, the idea that like produces like, Frazer cites
the "familiar application" in which an attempt is made to injure or to de-
stroy an enemy "by injuring or destroying an image of him" (35), or, in the
"amiable" sphere of "winning love," an arrow is dispatched into "the heart
of a clay image," thus "securing a woman's affection" (40). Here magic rests
overwhelmingly on a fallacious understanding of causality: like produces
like. If thunder accompanies rain, then to beget rain during a drought, we
can beat drums and roll boulders noisily down hills; if fertility produces
crops, and an eventual harvest, then we can copulate in the newly sown
fields and transfer our sexual energies to the precious, unpredictable seeds;
if fish must open their mouths and swallow our hooks or we don't catch
them, then we can open our own mouths in imitation of the fish and thus induce the effect we desire: like begets like.

Frazer notes that many examples of homeopathic magic are "supposed
to operate at long distance. Whatever doubts science may entertain as to the
possibility of action at a distance, magic has none; faith in telepathy is one
of its basic principles" (49). We might bear this in mind henceforward as a
kind of telepathy is often presupposed in prayer, and in two directions: we
can detect or perceive the presence of the ambient Almighty, and the Almighty can read our hearts, indeed can know precisely what is in them before we've uttered our supplication. However, as I've indicated, all of this is
but our initial stop along the way. Our grasp of magical behavior becomes
considerably more refined, considerably more sensitive to the human tendencies that draw it forth, as we focus upon the insights of a recent pivotal,
penetrating thinker. (I will punctuate the next few paragraphs with a wide
variety of parenthetical questions and comments designed to gesture in a
preliminary, hypothetical way toward an emergent, overall thesis.)

Writes Susanne Langer in her groundbreaking volume, *Philosophy in a
New Key* (1969, 40), "there is a primary need in man, which other creatures

probably do not have, and which actuates all his apparently unzoölogical aims, his wistful fancies, his consciousness of value, his utterly impractical enthusiasms, and his awareness of a 'beyond' filled with holiness." This basic, primary need, this "essential act of mind," she continues (41), is precisely "the need of symbolization" in the fullest, broadest, most encompassing sense. Accordingly, both "speech" and "ritual" are best understood as "symbolic transformations of experience," and "magic" as a descendant of these: "whatever purpose [its] practice may serve, its direct motivation is the desire to symbolize great conceptions. It is the overt action in which a rich and savage imagination automatically ends. Its origin is probably not practical at all, but ritualistic; its central aim is to symbolize a Presence, to aid in the formulation of a religious universe" (49). (Might ritual of prayer be the overt magical action whereby our "rich and savage imagination" strives to formulate a "religious universe," a universe in which an all-powerful Deity both rules and looks after his anxious, needy suppliants? Might the "Presence" that prayer strives to symbolize be the "Presence" of a supernatural parental figure unconsciously designed to replace the natural one from whom we were obliged to separate by the close of the early period? Might this be the "great conception?" Might prayer allow us to play it both ways: to be separate and to be bonded to the matrix all at the same time?) "Magic is never employed in a commonplace mood, like ordinary causal agency," observes Langer (1969, 49); "this fact belies the widely accepted belief that the 'method of magic' rests on mistaken view of causality." There is a deeper purpose here. "Magic . . . is not a method but a language," a "symbolic transformation of experience that no other medium can adequately express" (49). Like Mary Douglas, Langer looks to "psychoanalysis" (50) as a discipline that may help us significantly in grasping the nature and purpose of magical conduct.

These seminal remarks are richly developed in Langer's masterwork and one of the twentieth century's most remarkable philosophical volumes, *Mind: An Essay on Human Feeling* (1988). Here, Langer (289) reminds us that emotion is an aspect of perception, that our rational, intellectual lives and our emotional, psychological lives always go forward in tandem, that there is no such thing as a "cognitive state," that we are never without our cumulative, embodied histories. Mind, in the broadest and in the narrowest possible sense, is feeling. "Current memory," she observes, "seems to come nearest to the animalian pattern of hysteretic retention, the fact that each successive move in a total act changes the motivating conditions in the matrix just enough to induce the next advance, so the organism is influenced by its own past in the enactment of a complex impulse at least to consummation of, or—failing in that—to preparing a new international situation with subsequent potentialities." Such "cumulative retention," she goes on, "already exhibits the radical departure of *Homo* from the rest of the primate order; for it constitutes the primitive conceptual activity that is the substructure of mind, as the matrix of vital acts is the substructure of the organism. It is a subjective version of the unity of the act." (Might it be that our praying to a supernatural caregiver is the culmination of a long mnemonic process, a symbolic, ritualistic "move" that has a history? Might it be that its "matrix" is tied to the "internal situation" we confront early on as little ones when biological and emotional growth move us away from the primary caregiver to the wider world? Might religious supplication comprise the emotive enactment of a complex, defensive impulse which says, savagely and imaginatively, "I will deal with being on my own by creating and enjoying a symbolic version of the precious, supportive relationship upon which I've always relied?" We know from Winnicott [chapter 2] that transitional objects arise precisely in emotional, feeling response to the onset of separation from the matrix. Might the creation of such a transitional sphere be related causally, motivationally, feelingly to the onset of religious faith, supremely manifested in prayer? Winnicott (1971, xi) describes the transitional realm as one that harbors "the magic of imaginative, creative living." Might we take the hint?)

"Every perceived object, scene, and especially every expectation," declares Langer (292), "is imbued with fantasy elements, and those phantasms really have a stronger tendency to form systematic patterns, largely of a dramatic character, than factual impressions. The result is that human experience is a constant dialectic of sensory and imaginative activity—a making of scenes, acts, beings, intentions and realizations such as I believe animals do not encounter." (Might prayer, too, comprise a dialectic of "sensory and imaginative activity"? Might it embody a drama in which intention and expectation are imbued with fantasy, a "making of scenes"? If so, might the initial, rudimentary "sensorial element" be the onset and the establishment of a separate, independent existence, the actual, organismic truncation of an infantile symbiosis? And might the "imaginative element" be precisely the magical, symbolical one, the Winnicottian one that reestablishes the connection, and that gets under way in earnest as separation goes forward?) Writes Langer (292): "as fast as objective impingements strike our senses they become emotionally tinged and subjectified; and in a symbol-making brain like ours, every internal feeling tends to issue in a symbol which gives it objective status, even if only transiently. This is the hominid specialty that makes the gulf between man and beast, without any unbiological addition."

(If the early period is overwhelmingly bound up with parental care, with asking and receiving, might an objective precursor of prayer, or a naturalistic impingement that originatively engenders it, be exactly the asking and receiving that we do as little ones in our primitive, hominid, biological situation? In fact, might it not be exactly this asking and receiving that becomes "emotionally tinged" and subjectified in our "symbol-making brains" such that we subsequently and wishfully project it upon an imaginative, idealized, supernatural caregiver, a substitute parent whom we create out of our anxiety, our helplessness, our need—nay, out of our transference love and gratitude for the emotional, biological support, the emotional, biological nourishment we've received? Can we isolate the early, biological asking and receiving from the later, magical asking and receiving [prayer]? Dare we isolate it, that is, if we choose to understand ourselves?)

"Biographical memory," writes Langer in *Mind* (1988, 293), "is about the most complex mental function of ordinary human life, running like a spine through each individual history, and concatenating the human agent's mental acts into a life of the mind." (Might we view prayer accordingly, as an outgrowth of our "biographical memory" which "runs like a spine" through our "individual histories" and culminates ultimately in our mental experience as a whole? Everything else pertaining to our lives must be subsumed here, all the way back to the beginning where our biographies commence. Why would we make prayer an exception? If asking and receiving is the very spine of prayer, as it surely is, and if prayer is the very spine of faith, as it surely is, might not the biological asking and receiving that we actually do during the early period when such asking and receiving comprise the very core of our existence bear some relation to the asking and receiving we undertake later in prayer, a magical act in which a needy, helpless suppliant asks a supernatural, omnipotent provider for his "daily bread?" And further, if faith is prayer's magical parent-child, inextricably tied to supplication as both cause and effect, might not faith be simply the unconscious conviction that the early biological situation, now transformed, symbolified, and outwardly projected, still obtains?) "Ritual," states Langer (314), "is almost certainly older than narrative, because its materials are given in an entirely prehuman state of animal existence, with the rise of emotional, self-expressive movement. Such movement is unintentional, instinctive, perhaps even unconsciously performed. But it has two biological properties which destine it to become the stuff of symbolic rather than directly symptomatic expression: the tendency of habitual animal acts to become formalized, . . . and the fact that the expressive acts are visible to the performer and his fellows so that they, and he himself, experience the influence of a powerful suggestion."

(If "habitual animal acts" are formalized, indeed instinctually and even unconsciously formalized, and if such acts reside at the very heart of ritual, might not the ritual of prayer have something to do with our "habitual animal acts?" During the early period, our central "habitual animal act" is precisely asking and receiving. As dependent little ones we ask, and we receive from masterful, ministering big ones. Later, when we face an uncontrollable, unpredictable world as separate, individual beings, might we not be "unintentionally, instinctually, unconsciously" tempted to restore the earlier situation and thus provide ourselves with a masterful supernatural ally with whom and through whom we can face the unknown? Might we not feel more confident, more secure, in the embrace of such a magical alliance? In this way, might our asking and receiving in prayer ["Ask and ye shall receive"—Mark 11:24] imitate the asking and receiving that we do early on and thus trigger unconsciously through homeopathic magic a symbolic reestablishment of the original, protective, life-sustaining arrangement? Finally, if one's praying is visible to one's fellows such that it contains for them "a powerful suggestion," might not social, congregational supplication enacted by big ones who have successfully internalized a particular creed evoke an inclination to imitative magic from little ones who have already been indulging their creative, illusory, transitional tendencies [Winnicott] and who now stand at the threshold of independent existence, or autonomy?)

"Deep, unconscious desires and fantasies," maintains Langer (1988, 318–19), "are undoubtedly expressed in the symbolic gestures and words of magicians," as well as in "the world-wide, persistent belief in magic," its "ubiquitous, everyday acceptance." (Might "deep, unconscious desires and fantasies" lurk in the "symbolic gestures and words" of prayer? Might supplication itself be part of the "ubiquitous, world-wide belief in magic" and the supplicators themselves "magicians" in their own right?) "Magic," she continues, "is intense, awesome, but not an emotional outburst. It is in essence an expression of ideas, and as such is symbolic. Its ubiquity in the life of man stems from his specialization, the overactivity of his forebrain, which he feels as an exertion, and he looks to the external world for its effects because outward effects have been the result of all his felt impulses from the infancy of his life" (327). And then, "instinctive behavior normally leads to physical achievement. . . . Instinct is perseverative, conservative; the force of tradition is its modified version in mankind." (Might it be that the instinctive element in prayer is tied developmentally to the biological impulse toward attachment, and in particular the attachment that a man experiences during the actual infancy of his actual, individual life? Might such attachment comprise the unconscious element supplication strives to conserve? Might the religious traditions of the species be cunningly, defensively, protectively devoted to keeping this hominid securely bonded to a supernatural ally modeled on the good parental object, thus controlling and perhaps diminishing the anxiety that attends both separation from the matrix and the final separation of death? Might religion as a whole be the creation of an "overactive forebrain" prone to internalize experience and then project it outwardly again in an idealized form that fulfills unconscious wishes and negates unconscious fears?)

"Empathetic magic," states Langer (1988, 327), might be a "better term" for the magic that is "known in our anthropological literature as sympathetic." (She has Frazer's homeopathy in mind.) "The rationale of the practice appears to rest on a conceptual assumption which is probably unconscious today even in the lowest savage mentality, though its vestiges are still alive as the principle of such magic-making: the assumption that an act may be initiated by one being and picked up in its course by another." This feeling, she goes on (328), "would seem to stem from the earliest phases our existence as true human beings, when instinct still held the main rule not only over behavior but over subjective reactions as well. At that time the bonds among fellow men were animal-like, and as the Hominidae are a gregarious genus, moments of empathetic feeling may have been frequent and familiar. An impulse starting up in one person would be naturally picked up from the smallest bodily sign, as it appears to be among many subhuman beings from bees to birds. . . . The experience of empathy may have seemed as natural in that close-knit human society as it appears to be in a beehive or a school of herring today." In this way, "empathetical magical action is not imitation; it is an incentive move to start the desired action of the natural and supernatural beings that have its completion in their power. The relation between the intention and the realization of the act is supposed to be helped by imparting motivation to those divine or ghostly agents as some animals seem to pass an impulse from one ready agent to another." Magic, then, is "but a transference of each successive human behavioral impulse to the spirit or spirits hopefully adjured to consummate it." Is not the dyadic circularity of the infant-mother relationship but an extended moment of empathetic feeling? Is not empathy the very soul of early parenting? Might not prayer thus derive from instinctual behaviors picked up between people during the earliest phase of our actual lives, the phase in which the dependent little one asks the providential big one for succor, and the big one responds, empathetically reading the little one's smallest bodily sign? Might the animal-like bond that engenders empathetic magical conduct be, in the case of prayer, the frequent and familiar bonding of caregiver and child, the instinctual, biological foundation of our

existence, internalized deeply into our active forebrains whence it unconsciously elicits divers powerful, magical fantasies? Might prayer be precisely an "incentive move" on man's part to trigger a "desired action" in a
supernatural entity, a spirit, which has the longed-for completion of that
action in its power? And might that "desired action" be precisely the action
of love, and care, and protection, a magical, imitative version of the empathetic parental ministration we enjoyed early on and unconsciously crave
forever after? Is it this for which we ask? Is it this we hope to receive? Is this
the motivation we "transfer behaviorally" (and psychoanalytically)
through our prayerful impulses to the spirit we hopefully adjure, to the divine agent we call our Father?

As we've just seen, when Langer undertakes to illustrate the nature of
"empathetic magic" and its key role in the emergence of spirituality, of religious rituals and symbolizations, she turns to a "savage mentality," to the
primitive hominids of long ago, as well as to other species entirely: birds,
wolves, bees (1988, 327–28). Here again, in severely truncated form, are her
words: "that an act may be initiated by one being and picked up in its
course by another . . . would seem to stem from the earliest phases of our existence . . . when instinct still held the main rule not only over behavior but
over subjective reactions as well . . . [when] bonds among men were animal-like . . . [when] moments of empathetic feeling . . . were frequent and familiar . . . [when] an impulse starting up in one person would be naturally
picked up from the smallest bodily sign . . . [when] the experience of empathy . . . seemed natural . . . in close-knit human society" (328). Can anyone
fail to see that we have in this a vivid, striking, inadvertent description of
the first society, the first relationship between the dependent infant and the
responsive, succoring caregiver? We don't need Langer's savages and bees.
Exactly the sort of empathetic conduct she has in mind as a precursor of
magic is going on around us all the time, on an enormous scale, as countless
millions of parents simply attend to their offspring and as countless millions of offspring simply make their needs and wishes known to their parents.

Might it be that all this magic-inducing empathy is integrally related to
the ubiquity of magical beliefs "in the life of man" (327), and even more ger-
manely, to the ubiquity of man's religious beliefs, including prayer? Might
it be that people everywhere find themselves praying to an empathetic parent-God who can read their minds and hearts because they had such an
all-powerful, empathetic parent in their own lives? To express it another
way, might people at prayer be wishfully projecting their own precious, unconscious experience of parental empathy onto a supernatural Provider
who supposedly fathoms their "incentive moves" with His telepathic om-

nipotence? Or is all this merely a coincidence: millions of empathetically parented people worshipping a God who resembles an empathetic parent? What are the odds? The point is, what Langer calls "the essential act of mind" (1969, 41), namely "symbolization," is but one major facet of our mental inclinations; another is our tendency to project our unconscious needs and wishes into the world, in the full psychoanalytic sense of projection. Indeed, from the psychoanalytic angle, whenever we think or act we project. Our Langerian symbolizations are frequently loaded with our own peculiar culture-bound and instinct-driven aims and urges. Thus Langer is simply wrong when she holds (1969, 49) that magic is probably not practical at all in its origins but ritualistic: rituals point to purposes, be those purposes open or concealed. And she is wrong, too, when she suggests (1988, 328) that empathetic magic is not imitation but an "incentive move" to start the "desired action" of supernatural beings. As with symbols and projections, these two, imitations and incentives, go together: the imitation reflects or symbolizes the quality of the incentive move. As a component of an integrated ritualistic action, it cannot be teased out of it. To ask and to receive in prayer is to engage imitatively in a spiritual behavior (or an incentive move) which sits atop as it were a biological antecedent, namely asking and receiving during the early period of our lives. The mind-body rootedness of our infantile, biological dependency shapes and informs the nature of our ritualistic questing in prayer. It's not our fault, in case anyone is disappointed. It's just the nature of the beast.

RELIGION, MAGIC, AND THE FIRST SOCIETY

Edward Tylor's famous "minimum definition of religion" as a "belief in Spiritual Beings" ([1871] 1958, 8) places the emphasis upon the mind, upon concurrence with an all-determining conception, or idea. For this writer, and for other writers as well (see LaBarre 1970, 15), Tylor's definition points us firmly in the right direction. Belief in spiritual beings is the great global agent that distinguishes the religious from the nonreligious, fundamentally and forever. Those who believe in God, to express the matter familiarly, are at least minimally religious; those who don't believe in God are not, even though they may consider themselves religious in some popular, secular sense which generally means "in awe of the galaxies," or "fascinated by the mysteries of nature," or some such. The believers are potentially religious in the full sense, capable of moving utterly into the religious sphere if they are not there already. The nonbelievers, by contrast, must hold back; they just can't commit until a major shift in attitude occurs. So be it. For Émile Durkheim ([1912] 1976), however, the emphasis on mind, intellect, assent, concurrence draws the understanding of religion away from the realm in which it properly and supremely belongs, namely the social realm, society, with its laws, rules, morals, mores, customs, traditions—its collective, organized institutions. Durkheim did not believe the psychology of the individual could account for the emergence of societal forms. It helps enormously in grasping Durkheim's view to remember that he was not concerned with the ultimate origin of spiritual beings. Who knows where they ultimately come from? Who knows when, or how, or why they ultimately appear in human thought and culture. Who has removed the mists of time, looked into the distant past, and seen? For Durkheim, religion is there; it is a reality one discovers on the planet, either directly as one travels about, or indirectly as one reads and ponders. Having discovered it, what one finds in turn (Durkheim concentrated on primitive cultures) is that religion is made up of rites and observances designed to propitiate the gods and thus gain their support; that specific rites and observances are delegated to specific members of the community; that deities themselves have fixed, explicit functions to perform; and that religion exists primarily for the benefit of the social order and not for addressing the spiritual needs of the individual.

In this way, a society's "spiritual beings" turn out to be an integral facet of the overall system. "The religious," maintains Durkheim ([1912] 1976, 206), is identical with "the social." For "in a general way . . . a society has all that is necessary to arouse the sensation of the Divine in minds, merely by the power that it has over them; to its members it is what a God is to its worshippers." We immediately appreciate, of course, the accuracy of all this. Anyone who has been raised in a religious home, a religious tradition, or who has simply read and digested feelingly the work of Balzac, or Joyce, or Malamud, knows very well the extent to which religious beliefs and customs can determine a person's existence. The power of religion as a directive, social force is undeniable. Yet surely the psychology of the individual plays a crucial, causal role in the total picture. To make God equal society or society equal God finally raises more questions than it answers. Observes Malinowski (1954, 69): "the social share in religious enactment is a condition necessary but not sufficient. . . . Without the analysis of the individual mind, we cannot take one step in the understanding of religion." Thus the problem arises, how do we go about bringing the "individual mind" to Durkheim's social analysis? How are we to understand from an individual perspective that society's "power over its members" is "what a God is to its worshippers?"

The best way in is to concentrate not upon society as we usually think of it but upon the first society, the first social order the individual encounters, the first social reality he is obliged to negotiate, the first "fixed relation" he confronts during the course of his days. To express it as unoriginally as possible, we must begin at the beginning—and I don't mean at the beginning of the individual's career as opposed to the individual's societal enactments precisely because the distinction is otiose: we are social to the root; our individual and our social experiences are inextricably connected. The dyadic circularity of the infant-mother bond is the individual-social matrix of our bodily-emotional-psychological lives. Of overriding significance here is the appreciation that we internalize our experience during the early period. We take the object into our primitive body-ego, into our very tissues, our very guts, as well as into our growing minds, our growing forebrains. We set up the object as the scaffolding of our developing selves, as the mind-body presence on which we rely in utter life-or-death dependency and need. When we begin to separate from the object, from the life-supporting matrix of our early experience, and move toward the wider social world, we bring our internalizations with us; indeed, we use them to navigate (and to survive) the passage. The internalizing monad becomes the gradually socialized member of the community. Thus the tie to societal institutions is grounded in the tie to the object. The power of societal directives derives from the internalized bond to the caregiver. We are more or less hooked. There is a vital, dynamic continuity here which, if we ignore it, obfuscates our grasp of social forces and which, if we apprehend it, allows us to let in some light. Let me render the whole basic business from another, related angle.

Because social institutions (religion, education, occupation, marriage, family) come to replace the "institution" of the early parent-child interaction, because social institutions assume a parental role, we transfer to society the feelings, the energies, the needs, the wishes, the loyalties, the loves (and frequently the hatreds) that motivate us during the early period. The social realm becomes an extension of the inner realm; it draws us, compels us, holds us through the mind-body attachment that comprises the very core of the first relationship. To a significant, even determining degree, then, our relationship with society is a transferential one. "Culture," writes Roheim (1971, 122) in a classical psychoanalytic statement of the issue, "leads the libido into [acceptable] channels by the creation of substitute objects. The most important of these substitutions is a human being, the wife who replaces the mother. The basis of society is formed by these substitutions and therefore the psychology of growing up falls, in many respects, in line with the psychology of culture." And again (131), "civilization originates in delayed infancy and its function is security. It is a huge network of more or less successful attempts to protect mankind against the danger of object-loss, the colossal efforts made by a baby who is afraid of being left alone in the dark."

Accordingly, if our transferential relations with the social order turn out to be hostile or in some manner unhealthy, the social order does to us (or threatens to do to us) precisely what we dreaded early on as we interacted dependently with the parent: it confronts us with "the dark," with rejection, separation, isolation, even death, the bogeys we discovered as newcomers when parenting was either forestalled or malignant. To lose our place in society can feel like losing our place in the arms of the caregiver, which is why we tend generally to obey the rules, or to rebel in a fashion that will not result in ostracism, in the temporary or permanent loss of everyone and everything. Let's recall now Professor Durkheim's contention: "the power of society over its members" is "what a God is to its worshippers." The social and the religious go together because religious society inherits the first society, or functions as continuation of the initial social bond. The asking and the receiving that we do in prayer is but a small specific instance of the way in which our early biosocial situation moves toward the wider social world, its providential successor.

Winnicott's famous discussion of transitional objects (the blankie, the teddy, the raggedy ann) illustrates very well the process of cultural succession. Confronted with the closing stages of symbiosis, the newcomer (20–36 mos.) gravitates creatively and trustingly toward the potential space of the intermediate area. He lessens his emerging one-ness by engaging in illusory two-ness. He mitigates the terror of separate, individual existence by constructing an intimate relationship with a symbolic companion, or ally. He plays it both ways. He strikes out on his own, and he returns imaginatively to the kind of psychic fusion to which he's been accustomed. "With human beings," states Winnicott (1971, 108), "there can be no separation, only a threat of separation; and the threat is maximally or minimally traumatic according to the experience of the first separatings." However, "at the same time," Winnicott goes on (109), one can suggest that "separation is avoided by the filling in of the potential space with creative playing, with the use of symbols, and with all that eventually adds up to cultural life."

It is presently fashionable to position Winnicott's work in the post-Kantian philosophical tradition as further proof of our ineluctable human subjectivity. There is no reality, at least in the old, positivistic sense of the expression. When people enter into their illusory or intermediate zones, we must leave them alone. We must not question them, or push in. We must not invade their space. We must not say to the child, why are you talking to a piece of cloth? Nor may we say to the adult, the god to whom you pray is a childish invention of your wishful unconscious. Winnicott (1971, 2) describes his intermediate area as "the third part of the life of a human being" to which "inner reality and external life both contribute." But surely what we have here is better described, following Langer, as an old-fashioned turn on the part of a healthy child to old-fashioned magical thinking and acting based solidly on the child's unconscious wishes and fantasies, on his emotional, biographical memory of an emotional, biographical symbiosis, on his emerging inclination to formalize habitual animal behaviors (again, the symbiosis), and above all on his tendency to create straightforward empathetic magic out of empathetic parenting. Whether or not we question the child, we can see perfectly well as grown-ups what he is doing. There is no post-Kantian, epistemological problem here. There is no need to invent perceptual categories. Simple magical conduct is all that we have before us. As I will later contend, the epistemological question is sometimes broached tendentiously by Winnicott's followers as they struggle to legitimate their own religious leanings (see Jones 1991).

Let's remember, everything in the child's universe during these early stages is streaked with projective empathy, or as it is often unhelpfully termed, with animism. The objects of the external world exist in relation with the child. Clouds have round, puffy mouths and speak in deep-throated tones; birds give knowing, playful looks; trees hold out their leafy arms, offering protection and shelter; fish raise their scaled, sparkling backs, inviting wondrous, watery rides; and when for one reason or another the world becomes frightening, threatening, such projective empathetic creations immediately alter their flexible quality, or nature. Closer to home, and directly in reference to the overriding issue of symbiotic care-giving, its advent and its gradual decline, the child babbles with, whispers with, blankie or teddy while teddy or blankie listens empathetically and responds. Blankie's soft, supple folds or teddy's pudgy, furry lumps empathetically give or contour themselves to the child's handling, or touch. The child's smallest bodily communication is reflected in the object's shape, texture, posture, arrangement. The transitional substitute for the parent cuddles with the child, snuggles with the child; in an endless variety of ways, or projective moods, it is at one with the child—ready to play out endlessly the required symbolical games or scenes. The upshot is clear: transitional objects are magical objects designed to control and to alter reality in keeping with the wishes and needs of their youthful, omnipotent creator. They have a practical magical purpose which is open, transparent. They serve as symbolic substitutes for the relinquished parent, as transferential entities which point motivationally toward the major symbolic, cultural substitute for the receding parental figure, namely the godhead.

When Roheim (1971, 122) characterizes "the wife who replaces the mother" as civilization's chief substitute object, he errs. Not only does he leave one-half of the human species out of the equation, but he fails to appreciate the lengthy period that intervenes between the relinquishment of the caregiver and the begetting of a spouse. Not for everyone, of course, but for countless millions, it is the Deity who takes over the transitional realm; it is the Deity who instrumentally replaces the early, illusory, magical creations, and who provides the human creature with the inward security he craves as he assumes his separate existence in the world.

As for the Deity's inward, psychological origin, as for His primal tie to the early period generally and the first society particularly, a crucial, evidential item lurks in Robert Coles's spectacular volume, *The Spiritual Lives of Children* (1990, 40) where we learn that ninety percent of nearly three hundred youngsters between the ages of five and ten draw a simple human face when asked to render their personal conception of God. Surely we understand whence this face comes: it is the product of the empathetic parent-child interaction which resides at the foundation of religious magic as a whole. It begins to take shape as the nursing infant locks his eyes on the face of his empathetic provider. It begins to take shape as the caregiver's empathetic visage appears above the edge of the crib, or the playpen. It begins to take shape as he opens his mouth in his high chair to receive another spoonful of plums from the empathetic nourisher, his adored and adoring parental presence. Over and over again, thousands upon thousands of times during the early period, the little one looks into the empathetic face of the big one, and the big one looks back. Over and over again the child internalizes this empathetic visage, this face, as the bedrock of his own emerging identity, his trust in life, his very selfhood.

Permit me to recall a few remarks from this book's previous chapter. The genesis and the formation of the self derive from the initial mirroring experience with the mother. For the past few decades, this unique, remarkable aspect of our origins has been studied intensively by observers both within and without the psychoanalytic community and has come to be regarded generally as a central structural occurrence of our normal development. An inborn tendency on the part of the infant prompts him to seek out his mother's gaze and to do so regularly and for extended periods. The mother sets about exploiting this mutual, face-gazing activity. As eye-to-eye contact becomes frequent, and easily observed by the investigator, the mother's continual inclination to change her facial expression, as well as the quality of her vocalizing, emerges with striking clarity. Usually she smiles, and nods, and coos; sometimes in response to an infant frown, she frowns. In virtually every instance, the mother's facial and vocal behavior comprises an imitation of the baby's.

Accordingly, as the mother descends to the infant's level, she provides him with a particular kind of human mirror. She does not simply give the baby back his own self; she reinforces a portion of the baby's behavior in comparison with another portion. She gives the baby back not merely a part of what he is doing, but, in addition, something of her own. As Winnicott expresses the matter, "in individual . . . development *the precursor of the mirror is the mother's face*" (1971, 111). Of particular interest in this connection (I am no longer recalling chapter 2) is Winnicott's answer to his own question, "what does the baby see when he or she looks at the mother's face" (112)? He writes, "I am suggesting that, ordinarily, what the baby sees is himself or herself. In other words, the mother is looking at the baby and *what she looks like is related to what she sees there*" (112). Thus the process which engenders one's selfhood appears to go as follows, once again in Winnicott's aphoristic style: "when I look I am seen, so I exist" (114). Precisely in that "seen," precisely there, resides the jewel of parental empathy. Have we a variation upon the cogito in this? I was seen, therefore I am? Is it possible that Descartes missed, in his notorious monadic formulation, the empathetic, relational origin of his and everyone else's existence?

The point is, when one discovers God in Durkheim's social realm, one discovers Him as an extension of the empathetic object, as a version of the internalized caregiver one has seen and loved during the course of one's early experience. This is the personal, individual, subjective core of religion, and as the core, it can never be sundered from the theology, no matter how sophisticated and mature the theology may get. Religious belief can't be broken up, let alone gutted of its emotional foundation. God is there for those who believe in Him because the empathetic object is there. The very basis of religious feeling, the very root itself, is both infantile and naturalistic. Moreover, because the empathetic object is connected inextricably to the advent of one's selfhood, one's identity as a person, to find God in supplication, to detect His presence in prayer, feels exactly like finding or detecting the self, or better, like refinding or redetecting the self's origination in the face of the loving provider. The most important theological use of the term *face*, we learn from *The New Interpreter's Dictionary of the Bible*, is to indicate "the presence of God" (Buttrick 1962, V.2, 221). "Cause thy face to shine," cries the Psalmist (80:7). "Lead me on, Dear God! To see Thy face," cries the nineteenth-century Anglican preacher Frederick Faber (see Castle 1986, 20). Within the Judeo–Christian tradition of personal, subjective prayer, one meets his Lord "face to face." Indeed, unless such "face to face" contact occurs, unless one reaches the level of one's mind-body internalizations—the object, in short—one's supplication fails to attain its spiritual goal.

From exactly this angle we begin to appreciate in earnest the extent to which religious conviction, or faith, is a species of the uncanny. God is real, He feels real when we sense His presence, his "face," in unexpected or ritually induced moments of transformation, or grace, or gratitude, or mystical merger, because our primal, loving internalizations are real, are there. To discover the Lord is to discover revelationally the self because the self and the Lord are birthed in the same psychological soil: internalized attachment to the loving biological provider. We create the Almighty projectively out of our powerful transference love, our ever-active, lifelong wish for union, protection, and care. I suspect it was the uncanny quality of religious sensations that spooked William James ([1902] 1987, 467) into believing that something, "God, if you will," was actually out there, registering his prayers. James's wishful, unconscious projection was candidly based upon internalizations he could feel within himself. Because he ignored entirely the early stages of human experience, he could not go all the way back to the naturalistic wellsprings of "religious experience," including of course the experience of religious faith.

Concentration on the early period also helps us to refocus and put to very good use Malinowski's classic views on the nature of magical conduct. Malinowski (1954) pointed out more than half a century ago that magical acts, one and all, are "expressions of emotion," and more particularly, emotion bound up with the possession or the lack of power. Engaged in a series of practical actions, an individual often comes to what Malinowski calls "a gap" (79). The hunter loses his quarry, the sailor his breeze, the warrior his spear, or his strength. What does an individual do in such a case, "setting aside all magic and ritual?" Whether he is savage or civilized, in possession of magic or without it, his "nervous system and his whole organism drive him to some substitute activity." He is possessed by his idea of the desired end; he sees it and feels it. Hence, his "organism reproduces the acts suggested by the anticipations of hope." The individual who is swayed by impotent fury clenches his fists or imagines an attack upon his enemy. The lover who aches for the unattainable object sees her in visions or mentally addresses her. The disappointed hunter imagines the prey in his trap. Such behaviors are natural responses to frustrating situations and are based upon "a universal psycho-physiological mechanism" (79). They engender "extended expressions of emotion in act or word" which allow the individual to "forecast the images of wished-for results," and by doing that, to regain equilibrium and "harmony with life." Thus a "strong emotional experience which spends itself in a . . . subjective flow of images, words, or gestures" leaves a "very deep conviction of its reality." To the "primitive man," or to the "credulous and untutored" of all ages, the spontaneous spell or rite or belief, with its power "born of mental obsession," must appear as a "direct revelation" from an external, impersonal force.

Now, when one compares this "spontaneous ritual and verbiage of overflowing passion or desire" with "traditionally fixed magical ritual," one cannot but note a "striking resemblance" (80). The two products are "not independent of each other." Magical rituals "have been revealed to man" in those "passionate experiences which assail him in the impasses of his instinctive life and of his practical pursuits, in those gaps and breaches left in the ever-imperfect wall of culture which he erects between himself and the . . . temptations and dangers of his destiny" (81). We must recognize in this, writes Malinowski (1954, 81), "the very fountainhead of magical belief." Magic does not come "from the air" but from "experiences actually lived through." As for magic's persistence, its ability to survive failure and disappointment, it comes from the fact that positive cases always overshadow negative ones ("one gain easily outweighs several losses"). Also, those who espouse and practice magic, at least in "savage societies," are individuals of "great energy" and "outstanding personality," that is to say, individuals who are capable of swaying others to their view. In every "savage society" stories of a "big magician's wonderful cures or kills" form the "backbone of belief" and contribute to the pool of living myth which gives the authority of tradition to current formulas and rites.

To these hugely helpful and insightful remarks I would immediately add the following: the magical behaviors of the early period also derive from "experience actually lived through," also address a "gap," or "crisis," or "impasse of instinctive life." I am referring to the primal, traumatic experience of disruption that attends the passing of the symbiotic stage, that brings with it feelings of separation and smallness, and that reverberates powerfully and painfully in the psyche of many individuals for ever after, as Mahler suggested. The first natural, instinctive response to this crisis is the creative, imaginative turn to transitional objects, to magical, illusory creations that wishfully restore the dyadic circularity of the infantmother interaction. More directly in line with Malinowski's chosen terminology: having felt the gradual diminishment of the life-sustaining symbiosis and the accompanying anxiety of separation, the child's nervous system, the child's organism, drives him to an "obsessive, substitute activity" which permits him to enjoy the images of a "wished-for result" (reunion, remerger) and thereby to regain his equilibrium and "harmony with life."

Thus does the child address the initial gap in the "ever-imperfect wall of culture." Subsequently, as a developmental outgrowth of magical successes (or gains experienced early on, we have the customary turn to the socially sanctioned Deity, including of course the turn to individual, subjective prayer. Here, the basic biological arrangement of empathetic, symbiotic dependency is imitatively restored as the helpless one, the suppliant, asks the mighty one, the Lord, to be there for him, to guide him morally, to forgive his transgressions, to manifest His loving, caring presence (Langer's "incentive move" directed toward a "spirit"). As we will see increasingly from this point forward, the rite of prayer itself provides the suppliant with a "practical" result, with a successful employment of magic, in that it serves to recreate the emotional, psychological union the suppliant unconsciously craves. Simply to pray is to gain; simply to pray is to form a "backbone of belief"; simply to pray is to produce "a wonderful cure," a kind of miracle, or living "myth"; simply to pray establishes the pray-er as a magician in his own right. The ritual, as Frazer might have put it, imitates its end.

Roheim (1955) was among the first psychoanalysts to spy the connection between magic and the traumas of the early period, and like Malinowski, he drew upon his anthropological work in making his observations. "Magic must be rooted in the child-mother situation," he writes, "because in the beginning the environment simply means the mother. Therefore, wishing or manifesting the wish is the proper way to deal with the environment"(11). Roheim then goes on to say—and let us keep our eyes open for the gap we found in Malinowski—"the mother is not only known by the fact that she gratifies the wishes of the child. In truth, she would never be discovered were it not for the fact that there is a gap between desire and fulfillment." More specifically, "magic originates from the child's crying when he is abandoned and angry; it is not merely the expression of what actually takes place in the dual-unity situation, but is also a withdrawal of attachment from the object to the means by which the object is wooed, that is, from the mother to the word and back again to the mother" (12). Thus it is "obvious," asserts Roheim (44), "that we grow up via magic." We "pass through the pregenital to the genital phases of organization, and concurrently our mastery of our own body and of the environment increases. This is our own 'magic,' and it is analogous in some ways to the invocation of his own 'luonto' (or nature) by the Finnish wizard" (44).

In a series of key, summarizing sentences, Roheim states that magic is our "great reservoir of strength against frustration and defeat. Our first response to the frustrations of reality is magic, and without this belief in our own specific ability or magic, we cannot hold our own against the environment." The baby "does not know the limits of its power. It learns in time to recognize the parents as those who determine its fate, but in magic it denies this dependency. The ultimate denial of dependency comes from the all-powerful sorcerer who acts out the role which he once attributed to the projected images." While the "magical omnipotence fantasy of the child is a part of growing up, magic in the hands of an adult means a regression to an infantile fantasy" (45–46). Magic says, in the end, I refuse to give up my desires. With this we reach the core of our theoretical position and the threshold of our return to the literature of prayer.

The child-mother situation in which magic is rooted is primarily a situation of asking and receiving. Accordingly, it is the soil in which the magic of prayer takes root ("ask and ye shall receive" [Mark 11:24]). The infant's cry is the Ur-prayer, prayer in its original, presymbolic expression aimed directly at the caregiver upon whom the child's survival depends. Because maternal ministration is not perfect, because the child's requirements are not immediately met, the cry that summons the object becomes invested with power, intention, will, qualities with which the word also becomes invested as the symbolical mind begins to impinge upon primal, instinctual being. The magical formula for the emergence of prayer is clear: from the caregiver to the word and back again to the caregiver. In the beginning is the word because the word calls forth the empathetic parental relation from which both self and Deity are born. Nor do we relinquish our magical propensities as we mature. On the contrary, magic becomes in Roheim's words our "great reservoir of strength against frustration and defeat." Conjuring up imitatively through prayer an idealized, complexified version of the first relationship, we continue to rely upon a caring, empathetic Big One who hears and responds to our calls for succor and guidance. With the blessing of the social order—indeed, with its encouragement—we indulge our "infantile fantasy" of benign attachment to an omnipotent provider whenever the inclination to do so moves within us. We give up our "magical omnipotence" on the one hand, and we forge a personal, magical alliance with the Almighty on the other. Although we cannot control Him, we can perhaps touch His empathetic heart with our prayers.

THE MAGIC OF PRAYER

Individual subjective prayer in the Judeo–Christian tradition comprises a straightforward, even transparent instance of homeopathic or imitative magical behavior (like begets like) the inspiration of which is the ground of our biological existence, namely the first, providential relationship between parent and offspring. Supplication, the *sine qua non* of religious faith, is rooted in parental care, the life-or-death activity of the early period. Corporeal, mind-body experience gets transmuted to the spiritual plane. Over and over again, dozens of times each day, hundreds of times each week, thousands of times each month, for years, the little one calls upon the big one for succor, succor in an endless variety of forms, and the big one empathetically responds. The child is hungry; the child cries out. Then what happens? The caregiver arrives to nourish, to satiate. The child is injured; the child cries out. Then what happens? The caregiver arrives to soothe and "make better." The child is wet and uncomfortable; the child cries out. Then what happens? The caregiver arrives with dry garments and ministering hands. The child is frightened; the child cries out. Then what happens? The caregiver arrives to protect and reassure. The child is lonely; the child cries out. Then what happens? The caregiver arrives to cuddle and to coo. As Christopher Bollas (1987, 13–14) made clear to us in the previous chapter, the infant's experience of his first object, "the mother," is actually transformational in character: "it is undeniable that as the infant's other self, the mother transforms the baby's internal and external environment. . . . [She] is less significant and identifiable as an object than as a process that is identified with cumulative internal and external transformations."

If the infant is distressed, observed Bollas (1987, 33), the "resolution of discomfort is achieved by the apparition-like presence of the mother" who arrives in a timely, synchronous manner to remove the distress. Not only is the "pain of hunger" transformed "by mother's milk" into an experience of fullness, but the transformation is accomplished synchronously, as the hungry child makes his needs known. We may think of this as a primary transformation: emptiness, agony, and anger become fullness and contentment. Over and over again during life's initial stages, thousands upon thousands of times, the parent and the child are joined in such ministering, dyadic circularity—world without end. Stephen Mitchell (1988, 31), following Winnicott, puts the matter this way: the key feature of the facilitating environment provided by the mother is her "effort to shape the environment around the child's wishes, to intuit what the child wants and provide it. The infant's experience is one of scarcely missing a beat between desire and satisfaction, between the wish for the breast and its appearance, for example. The infant naturally assumes that his wishes produce the object of desire, that the breast, his blanket, in effect his entire world, is the product of his creation. The mother's provision and accommodation to the infant's wish create what Winnicott terms "the moment of illusion," the "foundation upon which a healthy self develops." Thus the early period of maternal care contains an endless series of "answered prayers." The big one, the "macrocosm" as it were, hovers over the little one, the "microcosm," and ministers to the little one's needs just as they arise. One would be hard-pressed to discover on the planet another example of physiological and emotional conditioning to compare with this one in both depth and duration. Our expectation that the macrocosm will respond to our requests for assistance is built into our perception from the start. Moreover, because mother and child achieve in the midst of their dyadic interactions what Daniel Stern (1985, 139) describes for us as "affect attunement," a mutual, empathetic, "telepathic" sensitivity to each other's moods and states, the big one's caring ministrations—nay the care-giving, care-receiving interactions as a whole—assume a magical, uncanny, clairvoyant quality, a sense of wondrous intimacy which serves as a foundation for subsequent spiritual encounters, such as prayerful communion. We must also bear in mind here the severity of the little one's needs, a severity that contributes powerfully to the depth of the conditioning just mentioned. The child is utterly dependent on the caregiver for his survival. Neglect means suffering or outright trauma at one end of the existential continuum, and death itself at the other.

It is hardly surprising that the experts describe the parent-child interaction in terms of addiction: "mother and offspring live in a biological state that has much in common with addiction," writes Winifred Gallagher (1992, 12). "When they are parted the infant does not just miss its mother; it experiences a physical and psychological withdrawal from a host of her sensory stimuli, not unlike the plight of a heroin addict who goes cold turkey." As the early period draws to a close during the third or the fourth year of life, the child begins to "transfer" to himself the "maternal care system" by turning it into the "self care system," and he does this through what is surely the most important of his internalizations, that of the good object (see Bollas 1987, 4). Increasingly he responds on his own and in a timely fashion to what he requires: food, drink, warmth, shelter. The caregiver of infancy disappears from the external world only to reappear in the child's internal world. As I have been suggesting all along, however, the switch is never complete. We handle the crisis of separation from the caregiver through the creation of substitute objects, a strategy that impels many of us toward the religious realm at the center of which reside the Deity and the rite of supplication. Perceptually, emotionally, we deposit a residue of the parental figure at the ground of the environment in which we have our being. The sacred and the spiritual, then, are loaded with early feelings of fusion and transformation, connection and change, union and the ineffable sense of the self's alteration. One is tied uncannily to an other who is numinous, magical because specific early memories rooted in the dynamic unconscious awaken affects that "say so." The attainment of grace in its myriad, endless shapes and forms (which arise chiefly from prayer), and in its ultimate mystery (amazing grace), is the sharp reinfusion of the infantile transformational process into the life of the changed or saved individual. The upshot is clear: as humans we discover through supplication a way to continue forever the asking and receiving which constitute the core of the first, life-sustaining relationship with the caregiver—world without end.

The Judeo–Christian tradition of individual, subjective prayer is ultimately petitionary in nature. In other words, asking the Almighty for help and support resides at its theological essence. "The heart of all prayer is petition," states Heiler in one place [1932] 1997, 17); and in another, "the free spontaneous petitionary prayer of the natural man exhibits the prototype of all prayer" ([1932] 1997, 1). "Whether we like it or not," declares C.H. Spurgeon, "asking is the rule of the Kingdom" (cited in Foster 1992, 179). "Petition is the heart of prayer," writes Cotter (1999, 13). "Prayer" is a "reverent petition to God," asserts Pruitt (2000, 1). The Judeo-Christian tradition of prayer, derived from both the Old and New Testaments, has always been "essentially petitionary," observes Elwell in *The Evangelical Dictionary of Biblical Theology* (1996, 622). "Prayer" is a "palpable thirst to ask," maintains Timothy Jones in *The Art of Prayer* (1997, 108). "Prayer" is a "trustful appeal for aid in our necessity," holds the great sixteenth-century theologian Zwingli (cited in Heiler [1932] 1997, 271). "Give us this day our daily bread," requests the Lord's Prayer. One could cite a thousand similar passages.

As for asking and receiving, we have the following: "One has only to ask the Father in order to receive what is needed," states Elwell (1996, 622), echoing Scripture. "Whatsoever ye shall ask in prayer, believing, ye shall receive," writes Hallesby ([1948] 1979, 22), quoting Matthew 21. "Petition" for "divine grace" is "freely bestowed," observes Heiler ([1932] 1997, 243). "God's power" is "capable of giving everything," maintains Guardini (1957, 63). "Asking is our staple diet," asserts Lindsay; "the spirit suffers when it is not fed the Bread of Life" (1996, 37). "Prayer is the spiritual practice of asking God for what you want and accepting that it has been done once you have made your request," suggests Joshua Stone in *Soul Psychology* (1999, 168); "God . . . hears and answers all prayers" (168). "Do you know why the mighty God of the universe chooses to answer prayer?" inquires Richard Foster. "It is because His children ask" (1992, 179). "Everything will be given to you," declares Cotter in *How to Pray* (1999, 14); you are merely claiming "what is already yours" (14). Our asking is itself "God's answering," holds Timothy Jones (1997, 110). The classical expression on the asking side of the equation has already been cited, of course: "Give us this day our daily bread." On the receiving side we have, from the

Twenty-third Psalm, "The Lord is my shepherd; I shall not want" (1–2). Taken together, these two lines contain the heart of the petitionary mindset.

One does not, however, go about his asking and receiving in an arbitrary, haphazard fashion. On the contrary, one undertakes his supplication by adopting a particular attitude, a particular psychological posture, or stance. And here we return to the materials, and to the queries, with which we opened this chapter many pages earlier. The wheel is coming full circle. We are about to behold the imitative magic of prayer in its raw, transparent expression. To demonstrate one's faith effectively through prayer, to find God, to be religious, one first of all adopts an attitude of utter dependency, utter helplessness, utter submission; one willfully attempts to get rid of one's will entirely. Allow me to recall in shortened form the key citations from the major theologians, and to enrich the discussion with one or two striking additions. "Helplessness," writes Hallesby ([1948] 1979, 13), "is unquestionably the first and the surest indication of a praying heart. . . . It calls from your heart to the heart of God" and constitutes "the very essence of prayer" (16), the "decisive factor" that makes us "more strongly dependent on Him" (21). At the ground of successful prayer, states Heiler ([1932] 1997, 258), is the "expression" of one's "weakness and dependency." One "submits" entirely to "God's will" and strives to make such "submission" a "permanent attitude" (268). The "feeling of dependence" is the "universal feeling" that "animates" the whole of humanity's relations with the Deity; "nowhere . . . is it revealed so clearly as in prayer" (77). "Man is ever conscious of his want and helplessness," maintains Guardini (1957, 78); "it is only right, therefore, that he should turn to the bountiful and almighty God, who is not only ready to give and to help, but greatly rejoices in it." Unless we "surrender without reservation" to the Creator, Guardini continues (64), unless we realize that our very existence depends upon God and His grace, our praying will be futile. While our powers are limited, God's are infinite. He allows us to breathe, to be, and above all to approach Him with "our needs" (134).

Identical views may be instantly discovered in the literature. Dependence upon and submission to the Almighty reside at the very core of Judaism (see Crim 1989, 385), and of Islam as well (see Hinnells 1991, 152). "Thy will be done," writes Cotter in *How to Pray* (1999, 28). The "value of surrender" in prayer is "extraordinary," declares Dossey in *Healing Words* (1993, 100–101). "God's plan involves daily dependence on Him. Without Him we can do nothing," maintains Lindsay in *Prayer That Moves Mountains* (1996, 37). Nor is it only one's inward attitude, or stance, that determines the emotional, psychological quality of one's supplication. One's bodily conduct may also enter integrally into the picture. For countless millions everywhere, inward dependency, helplessness, and submission are outwardly expressed by prayer's traditional ritualistic behaviors: suppliants kneel, bow down, close their eyes, fold their hands, even prostrate themselves entirely.

What is most remarkable, memorable, revelational about this theme of dependency, however, is the way in which it reflects, even mirrors explicitly, the original biological arrangement of empathetic caregiver and vulnerable child. "If you are a mother," asserts Hallesby ([1948] 1979, 14), "you will understand very readily this aspect of prayer. Your infant child cannot formulate in words a single petition to you. Yet the little one prays the best way he knows how. All he can do is cry, but you understand . . . his pleading cry. Moreover, the little one need not even cry. All you need to do is to see him in all his helpless dependence upon you, and a prayer touches your mother-heart. . . . He who is Father of all that is called mother and all that is called child in heaven and on earth deals with us in the same way." Thus we "cling" in our "helplessness" to the "spirit of prayer" whenever we pray (102). We know "the Lord is at our side," and therefore we do not feel "frightened" (119). When his own "little boy" comes to him with "round baby eyes" and asks for his assistance, Hallesby observes (121), he sees at once the manner in which everyone should approach the "heavenly Father" (121). We must "let our holy and almighty God care for us just as an infant surrenders himself to his mother's care" (20).

Heiler agrees. The feeling of "dependence and impotence" is the key to successful praying ([1932] 1997, 32), for we have no genuine power of our own: we are like "children who can do nothing" (36). It is precisely this childlike attitude, this childlike "trust and surrender," holds Heiler (130–31), that marks all the "eminent men" with "a genius for prayer," all the "great men of religion" (253). We "turn" to God "in prayer," writes Guardini (1957, 77), "as the child in distress turns to his mother." Jesus taught us, Guardini goes on (77), "that we should turn to the Father and ask Him" for our "daily bread," for the "necessities" of our "daily life." This is because the Almighty knows best what is "needful" for us. He knows how to look after us in every respect—in a word, how to "care" for us in our "helplessness" and "want" (78). "God will be found" in supplication, claims Buttrick (1994, 31), "not by our seeking" but "by a response . . . to One of whom we are dimly aware—as a child, half waking, responds to the mother who bends over him." When we pray, maintains Timothy Jones (1997, 107), "we take hold of His willingness to listen and move; we exercise our right as children to influence a loving parent." Cries Horatius Bonar in *The New Book of Christian Prayers* (see Castle 1986, 61): "Lead me by Thine own hand, choose out the path for me." Once again, a thousand similar quotations may be instantly found in the literature of prayer. The dependent child relying on the loving parent-God is probably the Western world's most common depiction of the supplicatory relationship. Thus a culminating question arises: why does successful prayer hinge so decisively upon the assumption of an infantile, childlike state, a state of dependence, helplessness, and submission that is persistently rendered in terms which recall the early child-parent interaction?

The answer resides in the formula for homeopathic or imitative magic: like begets like. If the suppliant recaptures attitudinally, psychologically, emotionally, affectively, the feeling of the early, dependent stage; if he assumes a physical posture that evokes associatively the relational realities of the early time (kneeling, bowing, prostration, indicating dependency, submission, even preambulation when walking was beyond one's capacities); if he projectively fashions a Deity who resembles a loving, succoring, empathetic parent, then (says his wishful unconscious) he will attain his treasured goal: to undo the past, to regain the colossal advantages that stem from an alliance with an all-powerful provider and protector, a devoted companion who is not only eager to assist him in his current circumstances but who empathetically, telepathically "reads" his innermost requirements before they are disclosed. The pray-er's original perception of the world, deeply internalized into his mind and body, will triumph over the realities that have emerged with his development: separation, smallness, mortality. As Malinowski (1954, 87) expresses it, magic is founded upon "the belief that hope cannot fail nor desire deceive. The theories of knowledge are dictated by logic, those of magic by *the association of ideas under the influence of desire*" (my emphasis). The rite of prayer attests on the one hand to the power of the past, to the preciousness of the first relationship, to the severity of our early needs, to the depth of our conditioning as little ones when asking and receiving were the order of the day, to the persistence of our longing for unconditional love and care—in a word, to the urgency of our unconscious requirements as they arise from the foundational years.

On the other hand, and just as significantly, the rite of supplication reflects the anxieties and the exigencies of the moment, the problematical now of the pray-er's existence, his present concerns, his present wishes (including those for the future), his present need for reassurance and support. Writes Walter Burkert, "rituals are complicated, ambivalent, and not seldom opaque even to those who practice them. . . . It makes more sense to see them as cultural attempts to make the 'facts of life' manageable and predictable; to perform an act of artificial social creation, as if to veil biology" (cited in Dennett 1997, 42). We don't have to puzzle very long to espy the biology that is veiled by supplication: separation from the matrix, the loss of infan-

tile omnipotence, dealing with a dangerous, unpredictable world, the inescapable facts of accident, illness, aging, and death. The point is, when Freud
(1964, 26) suggests that religion is based upon an "infantile model" he has
in mind the projective image of the mighty father looking out for the vulnerable child: "over each one of us there watches a benevolent providence
which is only seemingly stern and which will not suffer us to become a
plaything of the pitiless forces of nature."

As we may now appreciate, however, the wishful imposition is considerably more decisive, considerably more radical than that: the very asking
and receiving in which the infantile situation is rooted turn up through imitative magic at the heart of religious ritual. Religion is not merely based
imagistically on an infantile model; it actually recreates one in prayer. Suppliants act out their infantile wish. The biological foundation of infantile
life is transformed imitatively into the cornerstone of religious practice.
Moreover, because prayer and faith are inextricably connected, because
prayer is the cardinal expression of faith, because faith dies when prayer
ceases altogether, we discover in prayer the essential nature of faith, and it
is this: faith is the accompanying, inward assent to the practice of imitative,
supplicatory magic. If one does the magic, actually participates in it, actually entreats an empathetic, loving, parental spirit for succor in the conviction that such succor may emanate from the supernatural realm—if one
"means" all this, in short—then one has faith. Or again, if one persists in the
infantile expectation of macrocosmic response to one's entreaties for succor, and more, if one acts out this expectation through imitative,
supplicatory magic, then one has faith. Or still again, if one actively expresses, through supplicatory ritual, the unconscious wish for nurturant,
symbiotic contact with an idealized version of the original caregiver, then
one has faith. Or finally, in ten words, faith is the indulgence in a particular
kind of magic.

Two ancillary considerations arise here. First, when I suggest that prayer
is based upon an infantile model, I do not mean to imply that all prayers are
equal in their overall emotional quality. A sixteen-year-old's prayer for a
new convertible is one thing; a sixty-year-old's prayer for world peace is
another. Yet an infantile model resides at the foundation of both supplications. No matter how complex and multifaceted one's conception of the
Deity may become, no matter how selfless and sophisticated an overall, individual supplication may be, a prayer to an anthropomorphic God who
stands in a personal, loving relationship with the pray-er must always and
forever be based upon an infantile model. The reader may be thinking (and
this comprises my second consideration), "is not the putative infantile
model you offer but a metaphorical or symbolic representation, an imagi-

native depiction of spiritual reality designed merely to guide the suppliant toward an appropriate interaction with the Creator? Why must you insist on both its origination in infancy and its direct, causal connection to prayer?" I insist because religion goes all the way down, to the unconscious strata; I insist because prayer reaches into our primal, instinctual being; I insist because for countless millions the "faith-state," as James ([1902] 1987, 452) calls it, is a matter quite literally of life and death. The "faith-state," writes James (452), "is a biological as well as a psychological condition, and Tolstoy is absolutely accurate in classing faith among the forces *by which men live*. The total absence of it, anhedonia, means collapse." And again, "not God, but life, more life, a larger, richer, more satisfying life, is, in the last analysis, the end of religion" (453). Surely we understand with these citations in mind that the dependent suppliant's relationship to the succoring, empathetic Deity goes far, far deeper than metaphoric representations. The origins of prayer are tied integrally to the origins of our biological life—in a word, to our initial asking and receiving. We don't invent prayer; we act out our passionate, unconscious concerns as they are rooted in our elemental, mind-body experience. From the soil of what psychoanalysis calls "object relations" spring the psychodynamics of what religion calls "spiritual relations."

SUPPLICATORY MAGIC AT WORK

The appetite for symbiotic merger, the longing to undo the past, to dissolve ego boundaries and reunite with a succoring, all-powerful provider appears with striking, unmistakable clarity everywhere in the literature of supplication. How could it not? The passion for symbiotic union is but a variation on prayer's central figure, namely that of the helpless child crying out to the mighty parent-God. As Guardini (1957, 59) says, "the longing for union" is "to some degree present in every prayer which deserves the name." In this way, the most primitive, elemental asking and receiving that one enacts in prayer (which is faith's counterpart, remember) stems from the most primitive, elemental experience one undergoes early on, namely that of existing as an "organ" of the parent, that of being oneself and the caregiver too, that of possessing, as Bollas (1987, 13) puts it, an "other self." The "yearning for union," maintains Guardini (1957, 55), is the "first motive of prayer." Our "soul longs for union with God" (57). "We cannot be without Him" (55). When we pray, "our prayer becomes love, for love means seeking to be completely at one with another autonomous being" (58). Yet, Guardini goes on, "only God can create that nearness that fulfils our yearning" (58). Because desire for the Almighty is "inborn in human nature" (56), we "cry" for Him "again and again" (58). Guardini sums everything up with the assertion that "the yearning for God, for union, *is also prayer*" (56, my emphasis). Let's look further.

Prayer's "deepest motive," observes Heiler ([1932] 1997, 104), "is the burning desire of the heart which finds rest in blissful union with God." The "yearning for blessed union," Heiler continues (127), is capable of "overbearing" all the other "themes" which often find their way to supplication, namely "guilt, grace, and sin." In fully successful prayer, states Heiler (142), "God and the soul are bound together in indissoluble unity." The "contrast of subject and object which rules the soul's normal life is dissolved" (141). One "fuses with Him in deepest unity" (142). One encounters Him "face to face" (160). " 'God is in me and I am in Him,'" cries Elsa of Neustadt (cited in Heiler, 142). "I sink myself in Thee; I in thee, Thou in me," exclaims Tersteegen (cited in Heiler, 190). "Thou alone art my food and drink," pronounces Thomas À Kempis (cited in Heiler 209). "If I am not united with Thee I shall be forever unhappy," insists Gertrude of Hefta (cited in Heiler 209). "I am Thou and Thou art I," declare ecstatic, mystical pray-ers worldwide (see Heiler, 190). The famous historian Arnold Toynbee expresses it this way: "when prayer—the communion between human person and divine person—has been raised to its highest degree of spiritual intensity, it is transmuted into another kind of experience. At this higher spiritual level, personality is transcended, and, with it, the separateness that is personality's limitation. At this supra-personal spiritual height, the experience is unitive. At this height, God and man do not commune with each other because, at this height, they are identical" (cited in Frank 1998, 636).

Avows one of William James's ([1902] 1987, 359) subjects as he describes his sensations during heartfelt supplication, "I was immersed in the infinite ocean of God." Rabbi Irving Greenberg (1993, 142) renders it similarly: in "prayer," he announces, one has "an oceanic feeling of connectedness." Proclaims New Age guru Larry Dossey (1993, 114): "we have for so long defined ourselves as separate personalities that we have fallen into the hypnotic spell of believing that separation, not unity, is the underlying reality." However, adds Dossey, if we pray sincerely, if we allow ourselves to become "God-realized," we soon learn that love is a "living tissue of reality, a bond that unites us all," not merely to one another but to "a loving God" as well (115–16).

The powerful sense of merger with God achieved through supplication is often associated of course with mystical moments; yet we must not be distracted by this from prayer's common, basic, integral connection with union. "Mystical prayer," affirms Heiler ([1932] 1997, 225), is merely "the sublimest kind of prayer." Indeed, for the great saint and bishop of Geneva, Francis of Sales (ca 1600), "prayer and mystical theology are one and the same thing" (cited in Heiler 194). As Guardini (1957, 55) reminded us, the "yearning for union" is prayer's "first motive." We must also note here the intimate relationship between mystical prayer, with its dissolution of ego boundaries, and what James calls the faith-state. James writes ([1902] 1987, 382), "faith, says Tolstoy, is that by which men live. And *faith-state and mystic state are practically convertible terms*" (my emphasis). Earlier we defined faith as the accompanying inward assent to the practice of supplicatory magic, as the unconscious longing for symbiotic union with an idealized version of the caregiver. Accordingly, the psychology of faith is quintessentially expressed in the experience of mystical prayer. To feel merged with the Almighty, to have the sensation of ego boundaries dissolving, to emotionally become, or be, the divine Other, to achieve a perfect, mirroring, face-to-face union with an all-powerful provider is the psychological core of what we know generally as religious faith. When the infantile model—prayer, triggers its coincident infantile affect—faith, one enjoys in the present what one lost in the past: symbiotic fusion with a loving, succoring parental presence. Such is the power of supplicatory magic to accomplish its central goal, the reversal of time: maturity to infancy, death to birth—world without end.

Of special fascination is the extent to which the urge for prayerful union with God reflects, or better, picks up, the phenomenology of the early parent-child interaction. To adopt the infantile model is to reexperience psychologically key relational features of the intimate, primal bond. "As a true mother dedicates her life to the care of her children," writes Hallesby ([1948] 1979, 15), "so the eternal God in His infinite mercy has dedicated Himself externally to the care of His frail and erring children." Specific, clinical details on the biological side of this simile actually present themselves as wondrous, "spiritual" attributes on the religious, supplicatory side. Needless to say, if prayer recreates through imitative magic the asking and receiving of life's initial stages, as it surely does, then the appearance of those clinical traces in supplication is exactly what we should expect. We noted in the work of Bollas (1987), for example, the manner in which the caregiver transforms the infant's world. "It is undeniable," Bollas declares (13), "that as the infant's other self, the mother transforms the baby's internal and external environment." If the infant is distressed, Bollas continues (33), the "resolution of discomfort is achieved by the apparition-like presence of the mother" who arrives in a timely manner to remove the distress. Bollas calls this a "primary transformation": emptiness, agony, and anger become fullness and contentment.

Over and over again during life's opening stages—thousands upon thousands of times—the parent and the child are joined in such ministering, transformational encounters. When we discover the Lord through our supplications, Heiler informs us ([1932] 1997, 259), "a wonderful metamorphosis takes place." No longer do we feel uncertain about things; no longer do we have sensations of doubt or dread. Rather, we undergo "the blissful consciousness of *being cared for*" by a "protecting higher Power" (260, my emphasis). "Confidence, peace, hope, and trust" suffuse us, "often quite suddenly" [the descent of grace], and always, Heiler notes (259), involuntarily and unconsciously. Surely the reader will recognize at once what is going on here. The adoption of the supplicatory infantile model (as a response to some sort of crisis or stress) triggers the old transformational feelings which reside at the core of maternal ministration, maternal care. We undergo again the elemental transformational experience which we underwent thousands of times during the early period when our call to the succoring figure brought about a change in our internal and external environment. To pray is to reactivate both wishfully and adaptively a basic, primitive, biological conditioning that simply went too deep ever to be forgotten or relinquished. What served us well at the start will, through imitative magic, continue to serve us well along the way. We will ask, receive, and feel transformed—which is to say, better—by the time the process concludes.

Everywhere in the literature of supplication we come upon this theme. "God was present, though invisible," declares one of James's praying subjects; "he fell under no one of my senses, yet my consciousness perceived him." And then, "It was . . . as if my personality had been transformed by the presence of a *spiritual spirit*" ([1902] 1987, 69). We might recall here Bollas's (1987, 33) point that the mother's appearance in response to the infant's summons has an "apparition-like" quality. "Prayer has true transformative power," states Terry Taylor in *The Alchemy of Prayer* (1996, 15). Not only is God always there but just by connecting to Him through supplication we are altered alchemically, our leaden existence turning suddenly to gold. To pray, observes Guardini (1957, 7), is to shed our old being and enter into a nascent state of spiritual communion at the heart of which resides "the seed of a new life." This seed, this new life, says Guardini—and here is the early biological arrangement itself—"is given to us to tend as the new born child is given to the mother" (8). "Change me into Thyself," cries David of Augsburg (cited in Heiler [1932] 1997, 183). "Take me up and transform me," cries Peter of Acantara (cited in Heiler, 183). Clearly then, to supplicate, to indulge the infantile model of asking and receiving, is to engage in what Bollas (1987, 14–15) calls "the wide-ranging collective search for an object that is identified with the metamorphosis of the self." The suppliant "sustains the terms of the earliest object tie within a mythic structure" (the overall religious creed). The object is sought for its "function as a signifier of transformation." The quest is "to surrender to it as a medium that alters the self." In many instances of course a specific crisis sparks the longing for the transformational presence, as was exactly the case early on. Yet a basic, underlying motivation of prayer as a whole is to experience the hit of transformation over and over again, in one's daily existence, just as one experienced it regularly during the addictive, crisis-ridden phase of the initial parent-child interaction. As I earlier mentioned and as we may now see distinctly, the attainment of grace in its myriad, endless shapes and forms which arise chiefly from prayer marks the sharp reinfusion of the infantile transformational process into the life of the changed or saved individual. There is nothing miraculous or mysterious at work here. Grace is readily explained in purely naturalistic, psychoanalytic terms.

The early dyadic intercourse is loaded with periods of what Daniel Stern (1985, 124) described for us earlier (chapter 2) as affective attunement. Mother and infant interact on the same bodily and emotional wavelength; they share a common energy, a common telepathic understanding of each other's dispositions and requirements. Mother often knows baby's needs before baby makes them fully known through his squalling or squirming. The exquisite, empathetic, supersensitive connectivity that Langer (1988, 328) offered us in her crucial presentation of magic's hominid origins finds its classical expression right here, in life's opening biological arrangement when "moments of empathetic feeling" are "frequent and familiar," when "an impulse starting up in one person" is "naturally picked up" by another "from the smallest bodily sign" (329). Writes the psalmist, specifically in the context of supplication, of course: "Before a word is on my tongue, you know it completely, O Lord" (139:4). Writes Isaiah, also in the context of prayer and reflecting God's voice itself: "Before they call, I will answer: and while they yet are speaking, I will hear" (15.24). Writes Matthew in the New Testament, echoing the words of Christ, and still again in the context of asking and receiving: "Your Father knows before you ask Him" (6:8). According to Timothy Jones (1997, 139), "God may influence and speak without our knowing it." Moreover, even if our clumsy efforts to "address" Him are "akin to the child's first efforts to address his parent," God "hears them" through his "caring involvement" (67). God hears "all your uttered pleas," states Hallesby ([1948] 1979, 14), "from the very moment that you are seized with helplessness." He "becomes actively engaged at once in hearing and answering your prayers." Indeed, He knows what your supplication involves "before it has been formulated in words" because He knows exactly what "is present in the soul" (13).

Are we to regard it as merely coincidental that the parent-God whom we approach as helpless, dependent children possesses as one of His cardinal attributes the telepathic ability to read our requirements before we have pronounced them, exactly as the caregiver was able to do early on when our "incentive moves" (to use Langer's expression [1988, 328]), were made in the caregiver's direction? Think about it. At only one stage of our lives, during only one period of our actual experience, was an astonishing, telepathic arrangement like this one not only the case, but the norm. On a daily, hourly, even moment-to-moment basis, over and over again, thousands of times, for years the empathetic caregiver intuited or read (Stern 1985, 124) our requirements and responded to them in a timely, synchronous way. Our "smallest bodily sign" begot her attention. Before we even asked, she was there, caring for us. Later, when we pray as men and women, the very trait that defines the good object, the very telepathic ability that distinguishes her, turns out to be a central, defining feature of the parent-God to whom we turn for ministration, for care. He too knows all about our needs before we make them known to Him as His children. We are instructed by theologians to adopt an attitude of childlike dependency, to call upon the Almighty "as a child in distress turns to his mother" (Guardini 1957, 77), and when we do so we find that He possesses the very telepathic powers which our original caregiver possessed and exercised again and again on our behalf. Of course we don't have a coincidence here. We have the direct transference of an early, specific, interactional, biological trait from the natural caregiver to the supernatural parental presence who resides at the foundation of our magical, infantile, supplicatory model. Just as we can readily understand grace in naturalistic, psychoanalytic terms as the reinfusion of the infantile transformational process into the life of the "changed" individual, so we can understand naturalistically and psychoanalytically God's miraculous, telepathic powers as the suppliant's unconscious attribution of the good object's primary quality to the succoring, empathetic Creator who assumes her life-sustaining function. In the beginning was a caregiver who could magically fathom, and meet, our needs. Our wishful, religious inclinations will not allow such a one to slip away.

The virtually endless references to God's energies, God's powers, God's rays that appear in the literature of prayer comprise still another striking example of the way in which commentators transfer specific features of affective attunement (Stern) to the putative spiritual realm. As we have just seen, mother and infant interact telepathically; they share emotional, feeling states (Langer); their dyadic operations occur over and over again upon the same mind-body wavelength; like twin-stars revolving around each other, they dwell within the same energy field, experience the same gravitational pulls, the same universe of elemental forces. Both Jews and Christians have known God through the centuries as an energy or ray, states Karen Armstrong (1993, 220), who quotes St. Basil on this score: "It is by His energies that we know our God" (220). When we "experience these energies in prayer," Armstrong continues, "we [are] in some sense communing with God directly." Only through such prayer might one "hope to apprehend a Reality that transcended anything [one] could conceive" (220). "You may feel God in your heart," claims Terry Taylor (1996, 18) in *The Alchemy of Prayer*, "or you may experience God as a field of energy encompassing you." If one manages to align his spiritual vibrations with those of the Creator he will experience the entire surrounding universe as God (19). As we pray, maintains Dossey (1993, 104), we strive to bring our strong emotions to the task. We are absolutely still and concentrated at the surface, yet "like great surges of current in the ocean," our intentionality seeks Him out. If we can attune ourselves to the divine order we may well discover Him within. "Intercourse with God," says James ([1902] 1987, 416), is realized through prayer, and more specifically through "interior prayer," the only kind that counts: "wherever this interior prayer is lacking, there is no religion."

Exactly how does this interior prayer work? "Energy which but for prayer would be bound," explains James, "is by prayer set-free and operates in some part, be it objective or subjective, of the world of facts" (417). And again, in prayer "energy from on high flows in to meet demand, and becomes operative [;] . . . spiritual energy, which otherwise would slumber, does become active" (428). To pray, writes Hallesby ([1948] 1979, 12), "is nothing more than to lie in the sunshine of His grace," to "expose our distress" to "those healing rays." God knows exactly what we require, Hallesby goes on, because he has focused his "spiritual X-rays" upon us in preparation for our "light-ray treatment" (79). Our "quiet hours with God" should be "daily light-ray treatments of this kind" (79). "It is His divine presence," asserts Hallesby, "which *attunes* our distracted souls to prayer" (78, my emphasis), which readies us for his miraculous "Roentgen ray" (80). However, God's energies, God's rays, do not merely heal us, according to Hallesby; they empower us as well. A key feature of infantile symbiosis, of affective attunement, of linkage with the caregiver, emerges in this unforgettable context of metaphorical utterance: I am referring to the infant's sensation of vitality (Stern 1985, 157). God's rays, declares Hallesby (80), fill us with new power. As we turn to Him in prayer, "His omnipotence streams in upon us" (52). "This power," continues Hallesby, is "entirely independent of time and space." In the "very moment that we bend our knees to pray," the Lord's "power is transmitted" to us. "Here is an example," notes Hallesby, "of wireless transmission of power which transcends the dreams of the boldest inventor" (53). Not everyone, though, has access, notes Hallesby further: "only His own friends can establish contact with these inexhaustible sources of power" (53).

Let's get to the analytical essence of all this. What ostensibly "flows" between the supernatural and the suppliant is in reality the unconscious, feeling recollection of a vital, elemental, intimate relationship between the suppliant's nascent, genetical self and the attentive mothering figure whom he internalized into the unconscious core of his being. Because the one who prays cannot detect this relationship directly, he projects it (through the infantile model of prayer) onto the spiritual level and onto the energetic, powerful Other who supposedly resides there. Remember, the caregiver is attuned to our needs. When she responds empathetically to our requirements we are filled with wonderful, addictive sensations, vibrations, energies, with our feeling response to her powerful transformational capacities. Indeed, the caregiver's loving, feeling ministrations may be said to awaken us to life, to "switch us on," to make us "hum" with the feeling of existence itself. We are alive, we are vibrating, not simply because she was, but because she communicated her aliveness to us and through us, or conversely, because her rays, her energies, protected us from the deadness which the lack of mothering invariably engenders. Our genetic vitality must be nurtured into life. It is not God who does this but another human being. A person, not a god, has this power. We pray for many reasons, of course, and among them is the longing to get back to the source of our aliveness, to feel still again the indelible, primal "hit" we felt over and over again during the early time as the caregiver focused her loving energies, her loving rays, upon us. We eagerly adopt the infantile model of supplication because we would have that, again and again, just as we had it early on—world without end.

Can we not understand from this perspective why James would suggest that prayer is essentially feeling ([1902] 1987, 448) and that it adds "a new zest to life" (435)? As we may now appreciate, reconnecting to the source is full of zest because the source is ultimately the feeling of parental power and empathy, the loving vibrations that awakened us to the world. No wonder, then, that the literature of supplication consistently likens prayer to the *"heartbeat* of our life in God" (Hallesby [1948] 1979, 43, my emphasis), to the *"unconscious, indispensable breathing* of the religious spirit" (Heiler ([1932] 1997, xiv, my emphasis), to the *"breath* of God" who is *"closer"* to us "than any other being" (Guardini 1957, 25–26, my emphasis). Such images emerge from the ground of supplicatory theology because such images reflect the origination of our lives in symbiotic, affective attunement. James would no doubt disagree, relying as he does on "God, if you will" ([1902] 1987, 467). But then, my sacred duty, as described in chapter 1, is to offer an alternative to James's view, not to refute it.

Nothing illustrates the unconscious pull of supplication more vividly than the phenomenon of wordless prayer, not silent prayer, mind you, but wordless. Hallesby ([1948] 1979, 120) tells us in a section titled "Prayer without Words" that prayer "is really an attitude of our hearts towards God. As such it finds expression, at times in words and at times without words, precisely as when two people love each other." He then offers us the example of his own love for his own "little boy" who often wants simply to be with him; not to talk, not to play, but just to be with daddy (121). Hallesby goes on as follows: "we pray to God. We speak to Him about everything we have on our minds, concerning both others and ourselves." Yet "there come times" when we "have nothing more to tell" Him. "At such times," says Hallesby (121), "it is wonderful to say to God, 'May I be in Thy *presence*, Lord? I have nothing more to say to Thee, but I do love to be in Thy *presence*'" (my emphasis). When such a wordless prayerful purpose proves successful, Hallesby concludes, the suppliant becomes a prayer: "you yourself are a prayer to God at this moment" (122). Jane Redmont (1999, 4) puts it this way: "being *present* and knowing that God is *present*: sometimes that is all prayer is" (my emphasis). "Wordless prayer," claims Heiler ([1932] 1997, 177), is "a state of prayer" [think here on James's faith-state]. "The thought comes to us from very ancient times," Heiler continues, "that silence may be true prayer, the genuine Divine service." In fact, notes Heiler (178), "Madame Chantal defines prayer as 'a wordless breathing of love in the immediate *presence* of God' " (my emphasis). "Consciousness," writes Guardini (1957, 139), "seems on the whole completely outside faith." Accordingly, the very deepest inward prayer, the only sort that really counts, "moves, as it were, away from the spoken word and towards silence" (134), or alternatively, "beyond the duality of speech and silence" towards "fewer and fewer thoughts" (146).

Those who pray in this condition, Guardini notes (147), "may not even need any words or thoughts in order to establish the state of mind in which they experience the *presence* of God" (my emphasis). They simply approach God in order to be with Him (144). We might think of wordless prayer as a process of self-sustaining, self-gratifying inward attachment to an all-powerful supernatural presence, or more informally, as a magical, psychological "holding pattern." The suppliant wishfully recaptures the preverbal stage of his existence, the stage in which parent and offspring attune together quietly, silently, for delicious extended periods, half the day perhaps. They share one another's feeling states, one another's existence, presence, being—not toward a specific aim or purpose, not with a goal in mind, but simply to be together, to feel and to enjoy the presence of their treasured, symbiotic partnership. During the course of such silent, mutual attunement, the little one may feel himself empowered, filled with an inward, joyous aliveness, the hum, the vibration that attends his loving interaction with the caregiver. The longing to regain this primal mutuality, this primal sharing, this primal awareness of the other's presence, can run deep, all the way back to the beginning or very near the beginning as we recognize in Guardini's version of wordless supplication where "consciousness itself" is placed "outside faith," where the suppliant works to rid himself not only of his words but of his conceptions as well, his very thoughts (1957, 147). Here, the one who prays becomes imitatively, magically, in his wishful emotions, an organ of the other, a mere extension of the omnipotent big one into whom he merges, or perhaps disappears, as ego boundaries dissolve.

Guardini's description of wordless prayer calls to mind Mahler's description of life's opening weeks in which the neonate exists in an "autistic shell" oblivious of his own presence. To go around like this, actually to dwell in this self-induced trance-state for extended periods, would be to illustrate unforgettably the extremes to which the yearning for God's presence can take the devoted practitioner of prayer. Heiler, as we just observed, dubs wordless prayer a "state of prayer" ([1932] 1997, 177). Surely it is obvious that the prayer-state, as we may call it, and James's faith-state are closely, even inextricably related, particularly when we remind ourselves of James's ([1902] 1987, 382) view that mysticism and the faith-state amount to the same thing. To be with God, to be in His presence, is to be in the faith-state. In one word, the faith-state is a state of being held. What makes the whole business so extraordinary and so mysterious, needless to say, is that a spiritual entity accomplishes the holding! As we will see in a moment, the explanation for this is perfectly naturalistic and resides entirely in the realm of the uncanny.

Of equal and related significance is the notion that prayer, be it spoken or silent, is something in which the practitioner must immerse himself all the time. It is not sufficient that he pray only when he finds himself in trouble; on the contrary, true prayer, genuine prayer, never ceases. We must "incessantly receive into our lives," asserts Hallesby ([1948] 1979, 119), "a supply of spiritual power," for "nothing is so blessed as unbroken communication with our Lord." And again (120), we must "turn to God incessantly for a new and fresh supply of power from the realms of eternity. . . . Let your prayers ascent to Him constantly, audibly or silently, . . . throughout the day." Prayer, says Redmont (1999, 4), "is an ongoing . . . internal conversation, . . . a constant sense of the Divine, ineffable *presence*" (my emphasis). Our prayers, maintains Guardini (1957, 86), "should never cease to go out to God; not only as a call in distress but as a constant appeal to His creative might and sanctifying grace." In the "personal religion of the great saints," remarks Heiler ([1932] 1997, 106), "prayer is not limited to certain occasions; it becomes a *life of prayer*, a continuous hourly and daily intercourse with God." One's "entire life," cites Heiler (108) from the early Christian thinker Origen, becomes "one great continuous prayer." We don't have to puzzle very long over this remarkable material. Continuous prayer is simply the later, more differentiated, verbal expression of the longing that resides at the heart of wordless prayer, namely the longing for merger, the longing to be in God's presence uninterruptedly, to be receiving his energy, his power, his vibrations without stint, to be perpetually enjoying the inward attunement, the inward companionship and sense of attachment that mark the primal interaction with the loving, care-giving provider.

As Guardini says (1957, 56), the "yearning for God," the yearning for his face, "*is* prayer" (my emphasis). Thus "we cannot be without him" (57); we require Him; we hunger and thirst for Him (Heiler [1932] 1997, 209); we long to be with Him ceaselessly, just as we ceaselessly longed for the object early on; and through the imitative magic of prayer, through the continuous adoption of the infantile model, our desire for His presence is accomplished, over and over again—world without end. By praying continuously, of course, we "strengthen our faith," which means that we adopt the infantile model incessantly until the truth of our assertion, that God is there and available to us, becomes indisputable. In this way, we are continuously restored, made joyous, and also reassured; for if and when the question of His availability, or even of His existence, should arise, we will recall His persistent daily, hourly, moment-to-moment manifestations of Himself. We can depend upon His assistance. He will come when we ask Him to come. "Ask and ye shall receive" (Mark 11:24). Whatever imperfections may have inhered in our early child-parent interaction, they are redeemed by his endless, unconditional love. He is with us, abidingly, forever and forever, even in the midst of our departure from this life.

With the context firmly in mind, and with an eye to further enriching our grasp of prayer's psychological nature, let's examine a specific, high-quality guide to successful supplication. How are we to go about our praying? What should we expect, along the way and at the moment of truth when the Spirit joins us? Let's get down to the nitty-gritty of this magical business. If prayer "does not well up from our innermost being," writes

Guardini (1957, 1), we "had better not pray at all." Forced prayer is inadvisable. At the same time, successful prayer depends upon the "right attitude" (3), upon a firm decision to work at it, frequently and methodically. After all, we are attempting to plant the seed of a "new life" (8), and unless we plant that seed carefully our spiritual project will fail. We must always bear in mind, contends Guardini (8), that our new life, in contrast with our old, natural one of thoughts and feelings, is essentially hidden; in fact, "it rarely penetrates the threshold of cognition." Thus the danger ceaselessly lurks that we may "neglect it and allow it to be smothered." How can this be? That is, how can our new life be so precious to us, so crucial, so all-determining, and at the same time so indistinct, so elusive, so fragile? The answer lies in the fact that this life emanates from a spirit, from the "Holy Ghost" (8). It is given to us by God through the Holy Ghost, and we must tend to it as the mother tends to her "new-born child" (8).

As Guardini develops this theme over several pages, a number of key ideas and images emerge. Although we need God and God knows we need Him, "we cannot perceive" Him, or better, we cannot perceive Him "in the manner in which we perceive objects and people" (9). God is "more real than anything else," and yet He is also hidden. He can only be seen by "the inner eye of faith," by an "inner vision" that is "often clouded" (9). In this way, *we have no immediate experience of God*" (my emphasis). Only through faith may we find Him in "*the emptiness and darkness of the unknown*" (9, my emphasis). It is, notes Guardini (9), a "great mystery." To prepare ourselves for supplication, then, we must concentrate (12); we must "exclude everything else" (13) from our perception; we must "recall ourselves from everyone and everywhere" (14). God alone "matters now" (13). We must go inward until we can say with Moses, "Here am I" (Exod. 3:4) (15). Additionally, we must "awaken our inner attention" so that it "may focus itself on its object" (16). We must "clear the inner eye" so that it sees true (16). We must step into that "*mysterious place*" of supplication, into that "centre of power" where the self resides, where the self can "take root" and "be present" (18, my emphasis). What is this mysterious place? It is "the realm of the spirit," states Guardini (19), a realm where we may realize, in the midst of our concentration, that "God is here," the "Living," the "Holy," is here, and "here also am I" (21). Accomplishing this supplicatory task, observes our theological instructor, means drawing upon sources that lie deeper in our being, deeper than our "conscious faculties" (21). We have to find the depth of our "essential being" and dwell therein. Although God is in the world, He is not of the world. When we say He is present, He "remains hidden," even as we say it (22). Only our faith can sustain us as we "*journey out into this silent darkness*" (22, my emphasis), for God is "*as nobody and nothing is.*

He is from Himself and by reason of Himself" (24, my emphasis). His attributes, His vibration, His breath alone are in this world (25). He is that which can't be named, "the all-embracing ineffable," the "mystery of existence" (25). He has "no face as we understand it," no "body as we understand it" (26). He is indeed "beyond all human concept" (26). These are the strange, even astonishing truths which we must digest before we can successfully make the journey. Guardini then moves closer to the thing itself, recapitulating key notions in the context as he goes.

With the reader's permission, I will also head directly toward the goal in a series of brief, bold strokes. We withdraw to a secluded, silent place; there, we find the "sanctuary of our innermost heart" in which He is "always present" (35). We try to visualize his reality with our "inner eye" (27). Alone, concentrated, reverent and kneeling, we achieve what Guardini terms "the invisible attitude" (39). The experience of prayer now commences: we enter a void which is "vibrant with being" (43). We have the feeling He may be present in a "special, intimate way," close to us, abiding, even though "we cannot see Him" (43). Then comes the climax: "into this void of not-seeing, not-hearing and not experiencing, there may at times enter something, something inexpressible, yet significant—a hint of meaning amidst apparent nothingness which prevails over the nothingness" (44). What is this something that enters? What is it that is here, that is present with us? What is it that our "spiritual organs of perception" (45) are detecting? It is, declares Guardini (44), a breath, a vibration, both "faint and intangible" (44). And he continues, with great conviction: "this breath, this vibration is the manifestation of God; faint and intangible though it is, it can support our faith, so that we may persevere. If faith perseveres the void may suddenly be filled, for God is not a mere fantasy or idea, or feeling, but the all-pervading reality. He does not dwell above us indifferent in the blissful remoteness of celestial spheres, but with us" (44). If we want Him, if we wish to have Him in our lives, then we must ask for Him, seek for Him, cry out for Him in prayer (45). There is no other way. Prayer alone opens the door to the "reality of God" (45).

What we have here are vividly descriptive, detailed instructions for reaching, not the realm of the spirit but the realm of the uncanny. We withdraw from everyday reality; we choose some isolated, solitary spot; there, we turn our attention inward toward the sphere of our subjectivity; we concentrate intensively as we enter the void, the mysterious darkness, the deep psychic strata well below the threshold of our consciousness. What are we looking for in our "invisible attitude?" What is it that we seek in our withdrawn, concentrated condition, upon our knees, and reverently? We are seeking a hidden spirit with a nonordinary face and body, a concealed "centre of power" where the self, our self, not only takes root but enjoys its essential being. The God we struggle to detect is inextricably connected to us. Then what happens, if all goes well? We sense that we are not alone; something else is with us; something else is "present" (recall the significance of presence in wordless and continuous prayer). We detect, perhaps, a breath, or perhaps a vibration, and as Guardini says (44), it is enough to convince us that we've made contact. The elusive, hidden, mysterious spirit is there. As it turns out, of course, that spirit has always been there in a perfectly naturalistic, nonspiritual way. What we've contacted through our supplicatory action is the deeply internalized trace of a relationship, not an object or a thing, but a relationship. More specifically, we've rediscovered the origins of our selfhood in loving, affective, vibrational attunement, the intimate, awakening interaction from which our awareness of and participation in the world arose—a breath, a vibration, a hidden, mysterious, foundational presence, namely ourselves and the ministering other in face-to-face, life-sustaining symbiosis. Guardini's void is the great space of memory, the yawning past, the yawning unconscious region, the darkness from which we emerge through the succoring attentions of the apparitionlike parental figure who hovers over us in the beginning. "God will be found," suggests Buttrick (1994, 31), "by a response in prayer" to "One of whom we are dimly aware—as a child, half waking, responds to the mother who bends over him."

Guardini's guide to supplication returns us to the period of one common breathing, one common heartbeat, the period of not only face-to-face but breast-to-breast contact, of exquisitely sensitive empathetic bonding, of keen, almost subliminal registration of the smallest bodily sign, the tiniest shift of mood, of atmosphere, the tiniest stirring of infantile life, the breath, the vibration of our inchoate existence. This is what we are listening for in Guardini's void; this is what we may detect with our unclouded, inward organs of perception. Remember, Guardini asks us (77), as do other doctors of prayer, to approach the Lord as an infant in distress approaches his mother. We are instructed to return psychologically, attitudinally, perceptually, emotionally to specifically the first relationship from which our awareness of things arises. Clearly then, the principles of imitative magic lurk between the lines of Guardini's *Prayer in Practice*. His discussion comprises a kind of magical sequence directed at the self, a kind of self-magic, a kind of self-induced magical trance which entirely depends upon our empathy toward ourselves, upon our own keen listening, upon our own keen attention, upon our own keen ability to detect our essential, originative being, our own relational roots in the mysterious interactional past of intimate vibrations and breathings. The face of God is unique, mysterious, and

nonordinary because it is both a face and a mirror; it contains the unconscious lineaments of the relation in which the self was born; the body of
God is unique, mysterious, nonordinary because it reflects both a one-ness
and a two-ness, a process of symbiotic joining from which a single, living
creature emerges into personhood. "We have no immediate experience of
God" (9) because our experience is embedded in the mnemonic recesses of
our early existence, the strong time of life-giving nurturance and vitality
when the parental "centre of power" was our center, our universe, our all.
The point is, we are able to discover the supernatural realm because we've
been there all along; we've always existed in a realm of hidden, unseen
presences. Guardini is merely guiding us to our inner world of objects, to
the traces of elemental, affective attunement, to the "vibrations" which res-
onate at our deepest psychological levels, and when we find that place we
are persuaded and call it "God" because we have no other way of explaining it to ourselves. There is a mystery here, to be sure, but it is the mystery of
the uncanny, not of the supernatural. Everything involved in His coming,
everything without exception, has been in our minds and only in our minds
all along; or, to turn the coin over, there is nothing involved here outside of
ourselves.

A wide variety of statements, claims, mysteries, wonders, and unresolved theoretical issues are both illuminated and demystified from this
fresh, naturalistic standpoint. We continually hear, for example, that prayer
is rooted in the unconscious, reaches into the unconscious, arises from the
unconscious, engages the subconscious regions, and so forth, but we are
never offered anything specific on this score, never told how the process
works, never made aware of the connections. "Religious emotions in the pious man," states Heiler ([1932] 1997, 233), "force their way unconsciously
and unexpectedly, from evident and inner necessity, to expression in
prayer. Prayer wells up from the subconscious life of the soul." And again,
"men take over faith in God from the community in which they were born;
but how it first arose cannot here be discussed; doubtless it flowed from a
whole series of psychological forces" (3). "Prayer," asserts Dossey (1993,
18), is grounded in "the power of the unconscious instead of the conscious
mind"; it "need not always be 'thought' . . . 'unconscious prayer'is possible" (8). When we pray successfully, holds James ([1902] 1987, 195), "subconscious forces take the lead." One's "whole subconscious life," one's
"impulses, . . . faiths, . . . needs, . . . divinations," has "prepared the premises
of which [one's] consciousness now feels the weight of the result" (73). As
for those premises themselves, as for the "divine personages" which determine the attitudes and practices of the believer, including supplication of

course, they are "exerted by the instrumentality of pure ideas, of which nothing in the individual's past experience directly serves as a model" (55).

Let's get some specificity into this, and not merely specificity but concrete causation. The unconscious does indeed take the lead in supplication, does indeed exert its power, does indeed drive us forward motivationally with the force of an inner necessity, precisely because (*pace* James) there is something in our past experience which does directly serve as a model for our religious beliefs and behaviors, for the divine, supernatural personages we worshipfully approach (remember, prayer is the chief manifestation of faith and the central religious action): the early child-parent relationship directly serves as a model; in fact, that relationship is explicitly offered to us by theologians as the model for prayer. We are told to approach the Deity as helpless, dependent children seeking aid from a loving parental figure. And when we do this, when we fervently, reverentially, imaginatively, creatively, genuinely follow the instructions imposed on us, our wishful, imitative, magical yearning "carries us unconsciously away" (Heiler [1932] 1997, 194) and returns us to the early period and to the attunement, the affectivity, the mutuality, the symbiotic interaction in short, which reside at the heart of the early period. Accordingly, the subconscious forces which take the lead in prayer are linked directly to a specific unconscious region of our minds and lives. The "inner necessities" that prompt us to pray are the inner necessities of the first relationship from which our experience as people issues forth: the necessities of attachment, of care, of love, of vitality and security and general well-being. We pray because we yearn to discover all that again in the now of our existence; nay more, we pray because we want all that without the imperfections which generally characterize the early interaction as a whole. We crave a perfect parent-God who will love us unconditionally forever.

How can we be surprised that suppliants, when they actually discover this region of the unconscious, are filled with ecstasy, gratitude, and wonderment, not to mention a profound sensation of sacred mystery? How can we be surprised that they are utterly convinced that He is there and that He loves them? One of James's ([1902] 1987, 72) subjects declares, prototypically, "God surrounds me like the physical atmosphere. He is closer to me than my own breath. In Him literally I live and move and have my being." States another informant, again prototypically, "I have the sense of a presence, strong, and at the same time soothing, which hovers over me. Sometimes it seems to enwrap me with sustaining arms" (72). James (59) comments, "it is as if there were in the human consciousness a sense of reality, a feeling of objective presence, a perception of what we may call 'something there,' more deep and more general than any of the special and particular 'senses' by which the current psychology supposes existent realities to be originally revealed." But our psychology, now, understands this sense of reality rather well. The surrounding, soothing, powerful Divine, the strong, enwrapping, hovering presence, feels absolutely real to the fortunate suppliant because his deep, foundational internalizations are real, the mnemonic traces of his affective attunement are real, the emotional echoes of the succoring object are real. The suppliant has recontacted the ground of his existence, the ground of his amazing awakening into life, the elemental, primal birthing relationship in and through which he emerged into personhood, the joinings, the exchanges, the ministrations, the feelings which transpired between his dependent, nascent, vulnerable self and the caring provider who was actually there, the presence who actually hovered over him when he breathed, the arms that actually enwrapped him when he moved and "had his being."

Of course such an experience feels wondrous, numinous, nonordinary, otherworldly: it emanates from the mnemonic recesses of the mind, from the unconscious regions, which are worlds apart from one's everyday conscious mentation. The suppliant discovers himself in the realm of the uncanny, and because he can't see that, because he cannot grasp the psychological factors that triggered the experience and landed him there, he attributes the whole occurrence to the divine supernatural, to spiritual, esoteric "energies," to the mysterious workings of the mysterious Almighty, to "God, if you will," or some such. Kant remarked in a famous *mot* (cited in Heiler ([1932] 1997, 100) that prayer was "strictly a soliloquy," and when he did so he was both right and wrong. Prayer is indeed a soliloquy in that it involves no one and nothing outside of the individual who prays. At the same time, prayer evinces the trace of a relationship, a relationship that is acted out as the suppliant goes about his business. I am referring of course to the infantile model which resides at the foundation of the practice itself. There are two at the unconscious ground of prayer because there were two at the psychological place of prayer's origins. By the time the suppliant indulges his grown-up asking and receiving, these two, the vulnerable, needful infant and the ministering parental figure, have blended through the process of psychological internalization into one, one helpless, dependent suppliant beseeching his parent-God for His assistance and care. The spiritual wheel comes full circle, back to its biological origins as those origins now reside in the unconscious regions of the one who asks and receives, the one who still perceives the world as problematical, as dangerous, and who copes with his anxiety by fashioning through magic a version of the one who soothed him early on.

We often read in the literature that God dwells inside the suppliant: in the "deepest places of the one who prays," writes Heiler ([1932] 1997, 108), the "indwelling God" is at "work." One also reads that God is both in and out: "thou art wholly outside all creatures yet in all creatures," declares David of Augsburg (cited in Heiler, 186). Such assertive claims and sacred paradoxes, what we might call the ins and outs of God, ultimately comprise from the analytical angle a kind of slip, a kind of clue to an unperceived, underlying meaning. Specifically, they express the conceptual confusion that arises when the practitioner fails to espy the workings of internalization and projection. The Almighty does indeed dwell within; we have fashioned him from within through our magical efforts to recapture the early period and the life-sustaining alliance which forms its feeling, nurturing core. Indeed, we act out that magical effort every time we pray, every time we enter the realm of the uncanny, every time we come to Him as helpless, dependent infants and ask Him to assist us, to succor us in our need, just as we did early on when the magical provider, the magical presence, was there. And He also dwells "outside" because we have put Him outside projectively in our fervent attempt to deny the facts, to deny the loss of the original provider with whom we united utterly and upon whom we depended utterly in the beginning, in the strong symbiotic time which came eventually to comprise the realm of the uncanny.

One is generally advised by the experts on supplication to pray alone, at least part of the time; one is also advised to choose a suitable, powerful, spiritual place in which to address the Lord. Writes Heiler ([1932] 1997, 113) in a representative, summarizing passage: "John of Damascus calls solitude 'the mother of prayer.' All great men of prayer, mystics, and prophets, seek for solitude in prayer, whether it be in the distant mountains or the dark forest, in the quiet chamber or the dead of night." Cotter in *How to Pray* (1999, 39), and more specifically in a section called "Powerful Places for Prayer," urges us to enrich our "contact with the world of spirits" by supplicating at a location which can boost our spiritual energy, and he goes on to mention cathedrals, burial mounds, Jerusalem, Mt. Olympus, the Black Hills of South Dakota, and Lourdes. "Wherever you choose to enhance your prayer experience," Cotter (45) concludes, "the holiness and sacredness of a particular place is a matter of perception. It can be anywhere at all, . . . whatever helps you get in touch with the spiritual energy in all things." Choosing to pray alone in a "powerful place," to isolate oneself on the side of a mountain or in the cavernous nave of a great cathedral, is choosing to prime oneself for the performance of supplicatory magic, for the emotional and perceptual move into the realm of the uncanny, for the discovery of those mysterious unconscious regions whence the echo of the magical, symbiotic past emanates with a mystic allure. How much better will one's imitative magic work when one is alone in a setting that contains the right vibrations, that conduces to the achievement of one's astonishing aims: restoring the original parental presence in an idealized, complexified, wish-fulfilling form; reversing the flow of time; creating a precious, magical alliance with an omnipotent, supernatural provider whose loving attentions are focused squarely upon one's gratification and security, not merely for the moment, not merely for the current stage of one's earthly existence, but forever, for all eternity—world without end.

PATERNAL THEMES

The accent to this point has been upon merger, symbiosis, attunement, telepathy, transformation—what we can think of as the pre-Oedipal or preverbal underpinnings of prayer. It is time now to take up the more differentiated, symbolic, verbal, Oedipal side of the practice, to move toward the realm of the paternal as opposed to the maternal presence, bearing two things firmly in mind as we go. First, the paternal God is capable of absorbing, and does in fact fully absorb into His nature, all the emotional goals that we associate with the primary object, with the caregiver of the early period. In the concept of God the Father, writes Guardini (1957, 107) in an authoritative, summarizing statement, "earthly paternity and maternity and fused in perfect unity." When we turn to the Father we turn to Him intact, replete with the fulfillments and with the ongoing expectations that characterize and will continue to characterize our asking and receiving. Second, the developmental, maturational line between the Oedipal and pre-Oedipal is never perfectly clear, perfectly demarcated, or formed. We encounter ebbings and flowings, fluctuations and admixtures, a complexity, a continuum rather than a fixed, transparent category of growth. As is always the case when we deal with human behavior, we must listen patiently, relaxedly, closely, intuitively to the material we encounter, sensing its significance, its underlying meaning. If we pounce on it and try to swallow it whole, it will, I'm afraid, elude us. In this way, while the accent or perhaps the flavor of supplicatory magic changes, its basic, elemental aim does not change at all. The suppliant continues to act out his infantile longing for a personal, supportive relationship with a supernatural parental figure dedicated to addressing his innermost requirements, to loving him and looking after him as His own dependent, vulnerable child. Like still begets like. The regressive core fantasy of individual, subjective prayer asserts itself vigorously within the Oedipal realm.

Note, for example, the straightforward, projective anthropomorphism that inundates the literature. "Prayer," states Heiler ([1932] 1997, 38), "is real speech with another who is conceived as present, a Being represented after a human fashion." And he goes on, "man can pray only to a being like to man. To the thought of him who prays, God has the same psychological and especially the same psychical structure as man; he is created 'after his image and in his likeness'" (55). God is "person," pronounces Guardini (1957, 74). He is "able to listen," able to respond to man's needs. He "does not dwell in Olympian heights . . . indifferent to human existence"; on the contrary, "God is bountiful and generous. He cares for man, values and loves him" with all "earnestness" (74–75). Thus, concludes Guardini (109), "we pray, not to a vague concept of deity, but to a real and responsible God who has revealed Himself to us; who has told us His name. Our prayer must go out to Him." God answers our prayers, says Hallesby ([1948] 1979, 125), not simply because He loves us, but also because He understands "what each one of us needs." He gives us His gifts "of His own accord," out of his "goodness and mercy." To pray, then, is to feel soothed by "His tender heart" (143), "warmed by His love" (138), excited by "His plans" for both our earthly and our everlasting existence (138).

According to Timothy Jones (1997, 59), we require a God who can be near us, a present God who can "lend His ear" to our supplications. We want Him to be "actively involved" (62). We want "Someone" to be "really there" (62). Our goal is to be "familiar with Him," to tell Him our troubles and to hear what He "wants to say" to us (45). Asks Gerard Manley Hopkins of the Lord in poetical supplication, "dost Thou touch me afresh?" Then comes the answer: "Over again I feel Thy finger and find thee" (see Castle 1986, 17). Longfellow, also in verse, imagines God seeking after him, waiting patiently at the "gate" to be invited in, weathering the "gloomy mists" and "unhealthy dews" in His persistence to be of service to the unworthy poet (see Castle 1986, 17). The Reverend Tom Harpur in his volume *Prayer: The Hidden Fire* (1998, 42), describes the sensation he experiences while at prayer of feeling the "fringes" of God's "robe" brush against him. Commenting upon this anthropomorphism, Heiler ([1932] 1997, 30) remarks that it presupposes the development of the suppliant's "own self-consciousness," to which we would immediately add the following: the suppliant's self-consciousness, by the time he gains it, harbors an extensive and significantly unconscious history; it contains among other things the history of his separation from the caregiver and of his wishful, magical attempts to counteract that separation through the creation of substitute objects (Winnicott). Indeed, the infantile model which the practitioner adopts when he prays is designed explicitly to recall the time of infantile asking and receiving, the time during which the parental figure lavished upon him the bounty of parental care. The point is, God is person because only a person can be a parent. Making a man-God is simply part of making a parent-God, a wish-fulfilling caretaker, guide, and protector. He's human because our parents were. We transfer to Him the deeply internalized longings that arose in relation to them. The anthropomorphism of God, or God as man, is of absolutely no interest whatsoever to religion except as it comprises an integral facet of God as parent. We don't approach Him as one man approaches another man. We approach Him as a child approaches a parent.

Just listen to Heiler's ([1932] 1997, 61) representative, prototypical remarks. When we speak with Him "in prayer," he writes, we speak "as children with their parents." We find ourselves in "a social relation" which is also "a filial relation" (59). The Almighty is our kin, our father and our mother combined "into one and the same divine being" (60). The "idea of kinship," Heiler continues, quoting Farnell, "belongs to the alphabet of true prayer. In the liturgies of primitive peoples as of advanced religion the divinity is ordinarily addressed in the relations of kinship," as "mother," as "father" (59). "Art thou not our father? Are we not Thy children?" ask "Greeks, Romans, Indians, Sumerians, Egyptians, Assyrians, Hebrews, Australians, Pygmies, and Bantu peoples" (60–61), in short, "the world" (61). The "greatest spirits in the realm of religion," Heiler (97–98) maintains in conclusion, "have had the courage" to assert that the relation between "man and God" is precisely the same relation "that exists" between "parents and children." And "not only have they said that," they have "lived in such a relation. They have stood in innermost communion, in abiding fellowship with their God. God was to them *a real father*" (my emphasis). Note how Hallesby ([1948] 1979, 22) runs with this theme; note the incredible explicitness and vividness of his words, which lay the thing bare once and for all: "Jesus comes to a sinner, awakens him from his sleep of sin, converts him, forgives him his sins, and makes him His child. Then He takes the weak hand of the sinner and places it in His own strong, nail-pierced hand, and says: 'come now, I am going with you all the way and will bring you safe home to heaven.'" Hand in hand they go, off to life everlasting, the weak one, the "child," and the strong one, the devoted parent-God. It doesn't matter whether one is Christian, Jew, or Muslim: the longing for this kind of arrangement is the basic longing of religion. One's prayer is for this. One's faith is one's subscription to this infantile fantasy: eternal union with a loving provider.

Later Hallesby (112) writes, "it is the will of our heavenly Father that we should come to Him freely and confidently and make known our desires to

Him, just as we would have our children come freely and of their own accord and speak to us." And finally, in unforgettable syllables, Hallesby
(118) observes, "since children came into our home I have understood
[prayer] better than before. They come to me with all their failures, and they
have wonderful faith in the ability of their father to make everything right
again.... God is glad in a similar way when we, His little children, feel a desire to speak with Him about our daily experiences.... Speak, therefore,
with God.... He loves you" and is "waiting to hear." Thus does the infantile model of prayer lead directly to the fulfillment of its magical aim: "our
Father who art in heaven, hallowed be Thy name; Thy kingdom come; Thy
will be done, on earth as it is in heaven." This, precisely this, is what countless millions achieve when they go down on their knees in subjective, individual supplication. The parental presence they lost early on is restored to
them in an idealized, wish-fulfilling form. The magical alliance they were
obliged to relinquish is reestablished once again, and forever. No more separation from the matrix; no more gap; no more aloneness, insignificance,
mortality; rather, "kinship" with a loving, supernatural caregiver; "kinship" with a divine, omnipotent Being whose miraculous powers are able
to vanquish not only one's enemies, but death itself—world without end.
Thus religion's supreme ritual, prayer, of which faith itself is both the
engenderer and the ever-renewed offspring, is not only magical but effica-
ciously magical in its deepest, most secretive implications. It is not merely,
as Heiler ([1932] 1997, 38) says, that "in prayer man seeks to exercise a real
influence upon the divinity"; it is rather that an efficacy can reside, as Mary
Douglas (1984, 68) renders the issue, "in the action itself, in the assertions it
makes and the experiences which bear its imprinting." To pray is in itself to
accomplish the supreme goal of the magical action, namely attachment to,
union with, a supernatural parental entity; to pray is in itself to assert that
He exists and is there as a concerned Father; to pray is in itself to gain the illusory experience of His closeness, His precious, irreplaceable, indwelling
presence, His "tender heart," His firm, strong "hands," his security-inducing, spiritual "finger," in a word, the wondrous, vivid, uncanny
experience that recalls the reality of one's early imprinting.

Let's turn to the literature again in an effort to discover further details of
the suppliant's subjective asking and receiving. What do the experts in
prayer recommend? How must the suppliant proceed with the business after adopting a childlike, filial attitude and an appropriately reverential posture? Above all, prayer must come gushing spontaneously forth from the
heart, from one's "innermost being," as Guardini (1957, 1) puts it. "The
most vital prayer," he asserts, "is the one which springs unprompted from
the heart" (121). Prayer, writes Bishop Gregorios (1980, 49), "is not so much

an emotional-intellectual commitment of the will to someone who stands over against you as an allowing oneself to be trustingly carried, nourished, [and] supported by God." When we converse with Him, then, we must do so openly, candidly, intimately, giving everything, holding nothing back. "He who truly prays," maintains Heiler ([1932] 1997, 111), "cultivates prayer *for its own sake*. He seeks in it living nearness, and immediate touch, familiar intercourse and heartfelt communion with the Eternal" (my emphasis). Once again from Guardini (1957, 122): "prayer is an intimate form of speaking which should bear the mark of our personality. . . . [T]he language of prayer should be truly our own." Our prayers, states Hallesby ([1948] 1979, 44), should be "confidential conversations" with the Almighty, preferably conducted in some private place, in our own "secret prayer room," for example. We must allow God to lift us "up into His lap," to draw us "unto His own heart" so that we may be "close to Him," so that we may be able to "tell Him everything" (45). Directly addressing the reader, Hallesby (106) instructs him, "pray that you may become so confidential with Him that you can speak with Him about everything in your daily life. That is what He desires. . . . You will no doubt recall that it is written, 'In nothing be anxious; but in everything by prayer and supplication with thanksgiving let your requests be made known to God' (Philippians iv, 6, RV). He knows that it is in our daily lives that we most easily become anxious. . . . Therefore he beckons to us in a friendly way and says, 'Just bring all those little things to me; I am most willing to help you.'" Hallesby continues by reminding us that God "never tires" of listening to our prayers, of conversing with "His little children" (118). "Speak with Him," Hallesby concludes commandingly; "tell Him when you are happy. Let Him share your joy, for that is what He is waiting to do. Tell God when you are sad, when you are worried, when you do not know what to do, when you are anxious. He is waiting to hear about it because He loves you. This being the case, nothing is inconsequential or unimportant; everything that concerns you interests Him" (119).

In this intimate, emotional climate of verbal, supernatural exchanges we can readily understand the presence of this passage in Heiler ([1932] 1997, 98): "rational, philosophic thought destroys the presuppositions of a simple prayer. These are: faith in the anthropomorphic character of God, in His real presence, in His changeability, in the reality of personal communion with Him." Announces one of James's ([1902] 1987, 70) informants: "God is more real to me than any thought or thing or person. . . . I talk to him as a companion in prayer and praise, and our communion is delightful. He answers me again and again, often in words so clearly spoken that it seems my outer ear must have carried the tone, but generally in strong mental impressions. Usually a text of Scripture unfolds some new view of him and his love for me, and care for my safety. I could give hundreds of instances, in school matters, social problems, financial difficulties, etc. That he is mine and I am his never leaves me."

Another informant declares (71), "I feel as if God [is] with me, on the right side of me, singing and reading the Psalms with me.... And then I feel as if I could sit beside him, and put my arms around him, kiss him, etc." Although this statement appears "childish," comments James (71), it is "none the less valuable psychologically." When one decides to be with God through prayer, observes Timothy Jones (1997, 52), he must "slowly build a nest" for himself in his heart and stay there. Eventually, as his prayers find their way to His presence, he will be able to say to himself, "I am not alone" (62). It is through Heiler's ([1932] 1997, 111) remark, of course, that we discover the proper way into all this. One engages in close conversation with the Father not for some tangible benefit but "for its own sake." The action itself, the assertion it makes—these contain the magical efficacy, these provide the supplicant with the infantile experience he seeks, namely the experience of having a perfect supernatural parent upon whom he may utterly depend. Remember, we pour our hearts out endlessly to God, we tell Him without stint of our worries and cares, of our triumphs and disappointments, and of our love for His person, as His children, as His kin, as His dependent little ones addressing their attentive Father. Like begets like, or even better than like. What we had early on with some inevitable imperfections we'll now have again in a flawless, idealized form: a succoring, patient parental figure tirelessly devoted to our personal, idiosyncratic wishes and requirements, a parental figure whose attentions are focused entirely upon us, upon our troubles, our cares, our foibles, our fancies, not for today, not for tomorrow, not for next year or the year after that, but forever. Intimate, heartfelt, spontaneous verbal intercourse with God is a species of *transitional* behavior as Winnicott intends the term. It is a patent extension of the strategy one adopts in late infancy when separation from the caregiver prompts the creation of substitute objects to which one babbles endlessly in magical, fantastic fellowship.

When our culture offers us our Deity, our nurturant, life-sustaining Father, we know perfectly well what to do with Him in the putative supernatural sphere. We're experienced illusionists. We've been doing something similar with the internalized objects of our inner world and with their projective representations for some considerable time. We know all about dismantling the discomforts of existing alone. Can we be surprised that the actual or imagined loss of such magical, soothing intercourse with such an ideal, spiritual companion should fill certain worshippers with sensations of dread? "I have enjoyed communication with God," states one of James's ([1902] 1987, 70) subjects, and then, "of course the absence of such a being as this would be chaos. I cannot conceive of life without its presence." Another subject remarks that without the joy of prayer, life "would be a blank, a desert, a shoreless, trackless waste" (70–71). When the disruption of a magical, ritualistic activity threatens the practitioner with total disorder, total deprivation, with nothingness in short, we can be sure that its roots extend into the object relations of the infantile past. From the uncanny, unconscious regions arise the good sensations of prayer; and from those very regions arise the bad sensations too, the sensations we came originally to associate with the bad object, with the absence of care, of attention, of love: bad time, bad eternity; bad space, bad world—the "shoreless, trackless waste." How accurate is Guardini, then, when he suggests that the words we employ in our supplications reach down to the foundation of our lives. "Language," he declares (Guardini (1957, 212), "penetrates down to the roots of [the pray-er's] mental and emotional life; he thinks in it, feels in it; it is the vehicle of intercourse with his fellows and the means by which he learns the significance and use of all objects."

All objects indeed, including the first care-giving object of his primal experience. As Roheim (1955, 9) points out, "more than anything else, magic consists of incantations or of mere wishes which have been uttered. The child utters sounds and the mother reacts to the cry or the call of the babbling." Again, "magic must be rooted in the child-mother situation because in the beginning the environment means simply the mother. Therefore, wishing or manifesting the wish is the proper way to deal with the environment. . . . Magic originates from the child's crying when he is abandoned and angry; it is not merely the expression of what actually takes place in the dual-unity situation, but is also a withdrawal of attachment from the object to the means by which the object is wooed, that is, from the mother to the word and back again to the mother" (12). And finally, while the "magical omnipotence fantasy of the child is part of growing up, magic in the hands of an adult means a regression to an infantile fantasy" (45–46).[3]

The magic of individual, subjective prayer in the Judeo–Christian tradition is the supreme religious exemplification of this general necromantic formula: from the caregiver to the word and back again to the caregiver. Having attained the capacity to express our deepest feelings, our deepest longings, our deepest unconscious wishes and fears in symbolical form, we discover a projective perceptual reality which we can mold entirely to the heart's desire. We asked and we received as little ones. We cried out and the loving provider appeared. Now, as suppliants, as employers of infantile, imitative magic, we can do the same thing and expect similar results, only this time the arrangement proceeds perfectly, with a flawless parental figure at the center and with an eternity of union stretching blissfully away.

MIRACLES OF HEALING

We know from our history lessons that for millennia petitionary prayer has been associated with miracles of healing (see Elwell 1996, 622). Of course it has: just think of what suppliants believe. They are in direct communication with an omnipotent God who presents Himself as energy, as power, and who loves them unconditionally as their devoted, succoring parent. No wonder "the possibility of magic intervention," as Mary Douglas expresses it, "is always present in the mind of believers" (1984, 60). "His omnipotence streams in upon us," asserts Hallesby ([1948] 1979, 52). As we pray, we "establish contact with these inexhaustible sources of power" (53). As we encounter others, we "transmit to them by intercessory wireless that supernatural power which will enable them to lead victorious lives and which will put thanksgiving and joy into their hearts and upon their lips, instead of a series of disheartening defeats, bringing discouragement to both body and soul" (53–54). When Hallesby calls God "the Physician of our souls" (79), when he suggests that we should go to Him through prayer "like a patient to his doctor" (80), he simply takes the power-laden presuppositions of his dynamic theology to their logical, therapeutic conclusion.

Pruitt (2000) is also given to explicit medicinal similes in *Healed by Prayer*, a prototypical present-day treatise on magical supplication. For "true believers," he writes (10), there is no question that "God hears their prayers," that "healing prayer" is an "attainable, life-changing force." True believers are, after all, in the hands of "the Great Physician" Himself (19). Yet we must also think here on what suppliants have actually experienced and internalized during the early stages of their lives. Upon thousands of occasions they have experienced directly the caregiver's transformational capacity; upon thousands of occasions they have cried out for succorance and love, and the caregiver has appeared to meet their requirements, to heal them as it were. This powerful unconscious material is transferred to the Deity as an integral aspect of the infantile fantasy (faith) that resides at the ground of supplication as a whole. To express the matter from a slightly different angle, each time the believer prays, each time he performs the imitative magic which comprises supplication, he undergoes a little miracle of healing himself, a little miracle of improvement in, or perhaps amelioration of, his own mental, emotional, and physical condition. He feels better; his physician is there; his cry has been answered; his prayer has worked. It is not only logical for Hallesby and Pruitt to call God a physician; it is also feelingly, emotionally acceptable in that it establishes a metaphoric or symbolic connection between the internalized healer, the internal-ized transformer, and its projective extension into the supernatural realm of healing energies and salubrious rays. Accordingly, prayer's proven ability to restore and to strengthen the believer, something we read about incessantly in the newspaper these days (see Emery 2000), is rooted entirely in the powers of association and suggestion, both conscious and unconscious of course. The suppliant has attached himself to a loving, supernatural caregiver who loads him up with divine, healing vibrations. He is safe and secure in "everlasting arms" (Hallesby [1948] 1979, 122). He is with kin, with family, with his spiritual Father who protects and looks after him. And most of all, if an actual crisis is at hand, he does not have the sensation of being alone.

Surely when taken together these working associations and suggestions constitute in themselves a miraculous arrangement, or situation; surely they establish beyond question the efficacy of supplicatory magic; surely they oblige us to recognize in prayer not simply a "blissful, hallucinatory confusion" (Freud [1927]1964, 71), but a shrewd, adaptive conjuring, a skillful, life-enhancing sleight of mind capable of diminishing physical and emotional stress, whatever the cost to the participant's rationality. But what of notorious healings? What of the miraculous displays that transpire in revival tents and on television, for all to see? How do they fit in? They attest not only to an interest in, a curiosity about, miraculous events on the part of audiences everywhere; they attest also to a thirst for proof, a desire to be-hold the power of God with one's own eyes, a craving to know that He is real, that He is there, that one may confidently bring Him into one's own life as the mighty champion of one's own cause whatever it happens to be. Notorious, visible healings serve to banish any doubts one may have about the efficacy of the magic he is privately performing.

Here is a representative sequence from a semipublic session reported in Pruitt's (2000) collection of "inspirational true stories of the remarkable healing power of prayer." Carolyn has been involved in a terrible automobile accident. Her neck is broken, her body crushed and paralyzed. One day, several months after the event, her family gathers around her in prayer while selected members of the hospital staff look on. Carolyn "closes her eyes" and prays "harder than she had ever prayed in her life. Suddenly, halfway through the service," she opens her eyes "wide," and smiles "the biggest smile of her life" to me (60). When questioned, she declares "I heard Him. . . . He spoke to me. . . . I know he did. I felt a warm, almost burning sensation down my back. . . . I believe God has touched me" (60). Pruitt comments, "a great feeling of joy and thanksgiving spread over the room. . . . At that very moment, there was a feeling that God Himself was among" the participants. "Of course, Carolyn still could not move, but that didn't matter. She would. God had said so" (60–61). I suspect the reader can guess the final outcome of all this. A few days later Carolyn is wiggling her toes while everyone stands around her in tears. The patient knows He's there, is sure He's there, because the patient has recontacted in the midst of her dilemma the transformational healer who resides deep within the recesses of her own psyche. Her supplication returns her to the source, to the precious wellsprings of love at the foundation of her own life, her own natural existence. Her unshakeable faith in the Almighty marks the transference of this love to the flawless supernatural parent who shines down upon her. Thus her realistic "sense of something there," as James ([1902] 1987, 58) might put it, her belief that He has somehow touched her, turns out to be a manifestation of the uncanny, a reactivation of unconscious memory as such memory is willfully clutched in the hour of need.

Relying on Willa Cather in *The Art of Prayer*, Timothy Jones (1997, 207) suggests that miracles "seem to rest not so much upon faces or voices or healing power coming suddenly near to us from afar off, but upon our perceptions being made finer, so that for a moment our eyes can see and our ears can hear what is there about us always." How aptly this captures both the manner in which uncanny experiences tend generally to occur and the manner in which the uncanny emerges in the present case. God can be suddenly there for the sufferer because He's been there all along as an internalized good object born of good-enough parental care. To discover Him through prayer as one copes with tragedy is simply to put to an extreme, magical purpose "what is there about us always." It is the uncanny, not the supernatural, that is operative here. Dossey's popular volume, *Healing Words* (1993), strives to illuminate such miraculous, supplicatory experiences by way of Einstein's relativity, quantum mechanics, particles and waves, Bell's theorem, nonlocal interactions, and so forth, all of which items are for Dossey (xiii) exemplifications of what he calls, following Meister Eckhart, "the divine ineffable," the "Absolute," the mysterious, unfathomable order of God. Were James alive today and still interested in prayer, he might well be working along lines similar to those Dossey follows in *Healing Words*.

Just as I have no intention of attempting to disprove James's supernatural conclusions in *The Varieties of Religious Experience*, so I have no intention of attempting to refute the claims, the speculations, of Dossey's treatise, which I recommend to the reader. As I made clear at the outset, my purpose is solely to provide a naturalistic, psychological alternative to works that turn finally to "God, if you will" or to the "Absolute" in accounting for the nature and the wonders of supplicatory acts. The only thing we can be absolutely sure of in this fascinating area of human behavior is that the arguments over prayer's meaning will go on, and on. Unquestionably the most interesting utterance in Dossey for this author and this book is the one in which he suggests that prayer can heal by altering in the past the initial conditions which precipitated the disease in the present. Events at the subatomic level, Dossey (126) reasons, are completed only when they are observed; hence, if we pray about the past before we've actually observed it at the physical level we can alter it to our benefit. In explaining this further Dossey relies upon—of all things—Frazer's conception of contagious magic: things once in contact remain in contact forever. "Contagious magic," Dossey announces, "seems to be woven into the fabric of the universe!" (155) What can I say in the face of this bizarre material except that Dossey has chosen the wrong kind of magic. It is imitation, not contagion, that is at work in prayer. Suppliants do alter the past, not in fact but in fantasy. They negate the separation from the caregiver which is the past's chief early event, and they restore the caregiver in idealized form to their present lives, including their present illnesses. Indeed, each time the suppliant adopts the infantile model and prays he accomplishes this wish-fulfilling wonder. Each time he prays he performs a miracle which surpasses any physicalistic, mechanical marvel the savants of modern science may currently be dreaming on.

The classic example of a paternal or Oedipal supplication is of course the Lord's Prayer. Our Father is in heaven; the direction is skyward, vertical, not chthonic. We revere His sacred name, the differentiated, verbal expression of His presence, His essence. We wish for the advent of His kingdom on earth, an associative echo of kingship, of male rule, male order, and we underscore this wish both by the dutiful subordination of our will to His will and by a further turn to the heavenly regions, where absolute order reigns forever. We then express a primal, maternal, pre-Oedipal requirement: we ask to be fed, to be nourished; we beg for our bread. Continuing, we ask to be forgiven our trespasses, which is to say, our betrayals of conscience, of morality, the Commandments, the Mosaic tablet of laws, which provides the foundation of our social, relational, cultural life. As dutiful suppliants, we will reflect His merciful nature in our treatment of others, and even of those who have trespassed against us; as we see mercy in Him, we will accord it to our fellow creatures. We then implore His guidance in matters of good and evil; we ask Him to restrain us when temptations appear on our path. He is our strong parental presence, our deliverer, as we confront not only the moral weakness of our own characters but the evil of which His enemies are capable. We conclude by acknowledging his kingly, paternal, everlasting order, His omnipotence, His ability to rule the universe forever, and finally his praiseworthiness, his effulgence as our eternal rector and shield. The "Amen," which signifies essentially, "so be it," marks our willful commitment to the particulars of the supernatural relationship.

The classic example of a supplication in which Oedipal and pre-Oedipal themes are fused is of course the Twenty-third Psalm. Here, the suppliant views the Lord as his shepherd, as his careful guide and protector. Immediately thereafter he strikes a blended maternal and paternal note: he shall not want; the herdsman-master will accord him everything he requires in the way of emotional and physical nourishment. Dependent, submissive, following along, he will be made to lie down in green pastures, a striking maternal image of lushness, of leisurely feeding, chewing, swallowing, digesting, sleeping; he will be led to the still water, another vivid maternal image recalling both breast and womb, the peace of symbiosis, the mirrorlike, fluid surface in which the self is birthed into awareness, existence, being. Such care, such provision, such recollection of delicious maternal engendering and love restores the suppliant, pleases him soothingly in the innermost regions of his self-consciousness, his subjectivity, especially as those regions are ruffled by the tribulations of the journey. The suppliant returns to the paternal sphere. The shepherd is morally fastidious; he keeps his flock on stable, solid paths of righteousness; he is covetous of his unimpeachable identity, his name, his reputation as entirely dependable and prudent in his decisions for the route of his flock.

At this point (4), powerful Oedipal and pre-Oedipal preoccupations emerge together: although the suppliant must traverse the dark, harrowing valley of the shadow, although as a member of a mortal flock he must confront the final, terrifying separation of death, the reengulfment into the valley-womb whence he arose, he will be fearless because he will not be alone; the shepherd will be there with his supportive staff, with his protective rod; the suppliant will be reassured by the presence of his loyal, supernatural companion. Ultimately, there will be no separation. The employment of Oedipal and pre-Oedipal themes goes forward as the overall pastoral metaphorical framework fades off. The Lord will continue to nourish the suppliant even in the presence of those who stand against him. What a humiliation for his foes! The Lord will bless the suppliant, consecrate him, anoint his head with oil. What more could the suppliant want? He cries out. His cup runs over: both his inward spiritual requirements and his external physical requirements will not only be met but met in abundance; the breast is moist, full, dripping with life-sustaining nectar. Accordingly, the suppliant's future is sure to go well, is sure to contain goodness and mercy which will now follow the suppliant to the end as the suppliant originally followed the shepherd in the beginning. The suppliant will dwell in the house of the Lord, in the paternal temple, in the place of paternal worship, paternal power, and he will also dwell in the home, in that "house," in the maternal abode, in the place of rest and safety, in the protective womb of the elemental nourisher. Moreover, and lastly, he will not dwell there for a limited period; he will not be forced to relinquish his "house," his home, his place of cohabitation with the parental presence; on the contrary, he will dwell in that location forever. Ultimately again, there will be no separation—world without end.

These timeless prayers pull together many of the psychological themes with which we dealt in the context of this book as a whole and of this chapter in particular: paternal power, order, authority, protection, attachment to a sustaining force or energy; maternal merger, succorance, nourishment, affection, tenderness, security, the good object of the early period from whom we derive our foundational selfhood through loving attunement. Here are the central qualities, the central items, for which suppliants seek when they adopt the infantile model and discover through imitative magic a way to inwardly reunite with a flawless, emulative, idealized version of the original parent projected into the putative supernatural domain. For believers, needless to say, there is nothing "putative" about that domain; a supreme spiritual entity actually receives and answers their supplications. Moreover, millions of believers are convinced that the world will improve, even flourish, when everyone emulates their supplicatory behavior, when everyone finds his way to the realm of the spirit. For nonbelievers, by contrast, the realm of prayerful communion is a wishful illusion. While supplication may have some adaptive value, while it may work for those who cannot face reality, it ultimately gazes backwards, not forwards. It is problematic, not only because of its erroneous assumptions but also because of its tendency to forestall the genuine emotional and perceptual maturation of its practitioners. Let's look further into these combative, oppositional leanings, which appear to comprise, jointly, an integral aspect of our common humanity.

NOTES

1. The foregoing evaluations of Hallesby, Heiler, and Guardini are derived from the jacket and prefatory materials attached to their books. For biographical and bibliographical introductions to Hallesby, see Ferguson and Wright (1988,

286) in the reference section of this chapter; for Heiler, see Cross and Livingstone (1983, 451); for Guardini, see Glazier and Hellwig (1994, 363).

2. The reader may also be interested in the following quotation from *The Larousse Dictionary of Beliefs and Religion* (Goring 1994, 314): "it is clear that magic does have links with religion and that it takes seriously the supra-logical elements in the human mind."

3. Winnicott (1971, 47) also finds the origin of magic in the infant-mother relationship. He writes, "confidence in the mother makes an intermediate playground here, where the idea of magic originates, since the baby does to some extent *experience* omnipotence."

REFERENCES

Armstrong, K. 1993. *A History of God*. New York: Ballantine Books.

Bollas, C. 1987. *The Shadow of the Object: Psychoanalysis of the Unthought-Known*. London: Free Association Books.

Bowker, J., ed. 1997. *The Oxford Dictionary of World Religions*. New York: Oxford University Press.

Buttrick, G., ed. 1962. *The New Interpreter's Dictionary of the Bible*. Vol. 2. New York: Abingdon Press.

Buttrick, G. 1994. *So We Believe, So We Pray*. New York: Abingdon-Cokesbury Press.

Castle, T., ed. 1986. *The New Book of Christian Prayers*. New York: Crossroad Publishing Company.

Coles, R. 1990. *The Spiritual Lives of Children*. Boston: Houghton-Mifflin.

Cotter, P. 1999. *How to Pray: A Guide to Deeper Spiritual Fulfillment*. Boca Raton, Fla.: Globe Communications Corp.

Crim, K., ed. 1989. *The Perennial Dictionary of World Religions*. New York: Harper and Row.

Cross, F., and E. Livingstone, eds. 1983. *The Oxford Dictionary of the Christian Church*. New York: Oxford University Press.

Dennett, D. 1997. "Appraising Grace: What Evolutionary Good is God?" *The Sciences*, January–February, 39–45.

Doniger, W., ed. 1999. *Merriam-Webster's Encyclopedia of World Religions*. Springfield, Mass.: Merriam-Webster, Inc.

Dossey, L. 1993. *Healing Words: The Power of Prayer and the Practice of Medicine*. San Francisco: HarperSanFrancisco.

Douglas, M. [1970] 1996. *Natural Symbols: Explorations of Cosmology*. New York: Routledge.

Douglas, M. 1984. *Purity and Danger: An Analysis of the Concepts of Pollution and Taboo*. New York: Ark Paperbacks.

Durkheim, E. [1912] 1976. *The Elementary Forms of Religious Life*. Trans. J. Swain. Boston: Allen and Unwin.

Elwell, W., ed. 1996. *Evangelical Dictionary of Biblical Theology*. Grand Rapids, Mich.: Baker Books.

Emery, G. 2000. "Prescribing Prayer." *The National Post*, June 23, A17.

Ferguson, S. and D. Wright, eds. 1988. *The New Dictionary of Theology*. Leicester, England: Intervarsity Press.

Foster, R. 1992. *Prayer: Finding the Heart's True Home*. New York: HarperCollins.

Frank, L., ed. 1998. *Quotationary*. New York: Random House.

Frazer, J. [1900] 1959. *The Golden Bough*. New York: Mentor Books.

Freud, S. [1927] 1964. *The Future of an Illusion*. Trans. W. Robson-Scott. New York: Anchor Books.

Gallagher, W. 1992. "Motherless Child" *The Sciences*, July–August, 12–15.

Glazier, M. and M. Hellwig, eds. 1994. *The Modern Catholic Encyclopedia*. Collegeville, MN: The Liturgical Press.

Goring, R., ed. 1994. *The Larousse Dictionary of Beliefs and Religions*. New York: W.R. Chambers.

Greenberg, I. 1993. *The Jewish Way*. New York: Simon and Schuster.

Gregorious, P. 1980. "What Is Faith?" In *Faith and Science in an Unjust World."* Ed. R. Shin. Philadelphia: Fortress Press.

Guardini, R. 1957. *Prayer in Practice*. Trans. L. Loewenstein-Wertheim. London: Burns and Oates.

Hallesby, O. [1948] 1979. *Prayer*. Trans. C. Carlsen. Leicester, England: Intervarsity Press.

Harpur, T. 1998. *Prayer: The Hidden Fire*. Kelowna, British Columbia: Northstone Publications.

Heiler, F. [1932] 1997. *Prayer: A Study in the History and Psychology of Religion*. Oxford: Oxford University Press.

Hellwig, M. and M. Glazier, eds. 1994. *The Modern Catholica Encyclopedia*. Collegeville, MN: The Liturgical Press.

Hinnells, J., ed. 1991. *A Handbook of Living Religions*. London: Penguin Books.

Hinnells, J. ed. 1995. *The Penguin Dictionary of Religions*. London: Penguin Books.

Jacobs, L. 1995. *The Jewish Religion: A Companion*. New York: Oxford University Press.

James, W. [1902] 1987. *The Varieties of Religious Experience*. New York: Library of America.

Jones, J. 1991. *Contemporary Psychoanalysis and Religion*. New Haven: Yale University Press.

Jones, T. 1997. *The Art of Prayer: A Simple Guide*. New York: Ballantine Books.

LaBarre, W. 1970. *The Ghost Dance: Origins of Religion*. New York: Doubleday.

Langer, S. 1969. *Philosophy in a New Key: A Study in the Symbolism of Reason, Rite, and Art*. Cambridge: Harvard University Press.

Langer, S. 1988. *Mind: An Essay on Human Feeling*. Baltimore: Johns Hopkins University Press.

Lindsay, G. 1996. *Prayer That Moves Mountains*. Dallas: Christ for the Nations.

Livingstone, E. and F. Cross, eds. 1983. *The Oxford Dictionary of the Christian Church*. New York: Oxford University Press.

Malinowski, B. 1954. *Magic, Science, and Religion*. New York: Anchor Books.

Mauss, M. [1902] 1972. *A General Theory of Magic*. Trans. R. Brian. London: Routledge and Kegan Paul.

Mitchell, S. 1988. *Relational Concepts in Psychoanalysis*. Cambridge: Harvard University Press.

Neumann, E. 1970. *The Great Mother*. Trans. R. Manheim. Princeton: Princeton University Press.

Noss, D. and J. Noss, 1990. *A History of the World's Religions*. New York: Macmillan.

Pruitt, J. 2000. *Healed by Prayer*. New York: Avon Books.

Redmont, J. 1999. *When in Doubt, Sing: Prayer in Daily Life*. New York: HarperCollins.

Rizzuto, A.-M. 1979. *The Birth of the Living God: A Psychoanalytic Study*. Chicago: University of Chicago Press.

Roheim, G. 1955. *Magic and Schizophrenia*. Bloomington: Indiana University Press.

Roheim, G. 1971. *The Origin and Function of Culture*. New York: Doubleday.

Smith, J., ed. 1995. *The HarperCollins Dictionary of Religion*. New York: HarperCollins.

Stern, D. 1985. *The Interpersonal World of the Infant*. New York: Basic Books.

Stone, J. 1999. *Soul Psychology: How to Clear Negative Emotions and Spiritualize Your Life*. New York: Ballantine Books.

Taylor, T. 1996. *The Alchemy of Prayer*. Tiburon, Calif.: H.J. Kramer, Inc.

Tylor, E. [1871] 1958. *The Origins of Culture*. Vol. 2. New York: Harper and Brothers.

Winnicott, D. 1971. *Playing and Reality*. New York: Basic Books.

Winward, S. 1961. *Teach Yourself How to Pray*. London: English Universities Press.

Wright, D. and S. Ferguson, eds. 1998. *The New Dictionary of Theology*. Leicester, England: Intervarsity Press.

CHAPTER 4

CONCLUSION: THE UNCHANGING NATURE OF RELIGIOUS FAITH

During the past half-century, a sea change has occurred in the psychology of religion, largely as a result of Winnicott's (1971) theoretical efforts. No longer an obsessional, neurotic, regressive practice (as Freud [1964] viewed the matter), religion has become a normative, adaptive, transitional behavior which helps the individual to cope with, to make sense of, the realities he confronts on the planet as he moves from one stage of psychosexual development to the next. Religion transpires in the imaginative, playful, "intermediate area of experiencing" (Winnicott 1971, 2). As healthy, life-enhancing "illusion" (Winnicott 1971, 3), it is akin to "art" in particular (Winnicott 1971, 3; Meissner 1984, 168; Jones 1991, 45) and to the creations of "culture" in general (Rizzuto 1979, 209). It is neither "objective" nor "subjective," but resides in that vast zone "between objectivity and subjectivity" (Winnicott 1971, 20). Thus "the experience of faith," as Meissner (1984, 178) expresses it, "represents a realm in which the subjective and the objective interpenetrate." Much of this, of course, rings true. Religion is certainly a unique, astounding product of the human imagination, a monument to the complexity, to the ingenuity of the human mind. It certainly does make life bearable, even joyous, coherent, and secure, for millions upon millions of people. As James ([1902] 1987, 435) was fond of pointing out, religion works. However, to conflate religion with art, with the cultural creations of the "intermediate area of experiencing," to situate it somewhere on a philosophical, perceptual continuum between subjectivity and objectivity, raises a number of serious issues to which we must address ourselves immediately.

Art makes no truth-claims; it never has, and it never will—not one. Keats's nightingale will never sing; Blake's tiger will never roam the forest. Michelangelo's David will never strike Goliath with a stone; Monet's water lilies, floating beneath a bridge, will never see the close of the soft, spring light. Shortly after Othello kills himself upon the stage, the actor who played him takes off his makeup, changes into his street clothes, and goes home. Art may be symbolically true, of course; it may "hold the mirror to nature," as Shakespeare has it; it may tell us all sorts of important things about who and what we are; but it is never literally true, rigorously true, objectively true; it lives entirely and forever in the imaginal land of metaphor. Only a young child or a madman believes in the objective truth of an *objet d'art*. Religion, by contrast, makes truth-claims; in fact, it makes no other kind; it is totally objectivist in its outlook; it repudiates the attachment of any subjectivity to its central claims, the claims by which and through which it lives as a cultural institution. Observes the distinguished theologian John Polkinghorne (1998, 116–17) in his celebrated Yale lectures, "God is not just one entity among the many entities of the world, available to be picked out and examined in isolation. The divine presence is the ground of the world's being, and the Creator is party to every occurrence." One would be very hard-pressed indeed to tease a subjective element out of this. Polkinghorne makes the matter as plain as the nose on one's face: God is real, absolutely and finally real, real in every conceivable sense, more real than anything else in the world. Moreover, one may say with complete, unqualified assurance that Polkinghorne's attitude is shared by religious people everywhere; belief in the absolute reality of God is ubiquitous among the faithful. Any disagreement, any dissent, any qualification of this basic tenet indicates one thing and one thing only: disbelief.

Listen with this in mind to Winnicott's (1971, 2–3) famous description of the "intermediate area," and note in particular his closing reference to art and religion: "the third part of the life of a human being, a part we cannot ignore, is an intermediate area of *experiencing*, to which inner reality and external life both contribute. It is an area that is not challenged, because no claim is made on its behalf except that it shall exist as a resting-place for the individual engaged in the perpetual human task of keeping inner and outer reality separate yet interrelated. . . . I am here staking a claim for an intermediate state between a baby's inability and his growing ability to recognize and accept reality. I am therefore studying the substance of *illusion*, that which is allowed to the infant, and which in adult life is inherent in art and religion." What was that again? "It is an area *that is not challenged* because *no claim is made on its behalf* except that it shall exist as resting-place" (my emphasis)? Surely this is off the mark, unless Winnicott is referring to the inhabitants of some other planet. As far as earthlings are concerned, while no claims may be made on art's behalf, they certainly are made on religion's behalf. Indeed, people routinely go to war to defend or to assert their religious claims. They sack Jerusalem over their claims; they burn dissenters at the stake, or tear them limb from limb; they drop bombs on each other; they propagandize, they proselytize, they go off on missionary journeys; they would rather die than renounce their religious claims; death itself is preferable to the betrayal of God's word, whatever that word happens to be at some particular moment in some particular place. More claims have been made on behalf of religion than on behalf of anything else in the history of the world; it isn't even close. Some resting-place!

Granted, people may feel strongly one way or the other about the work of, say, Henri Matisse, but they don't kill themselves over the matter, that is, unless they are willing to put at risk their reputations in artistic circles. It is equally mistaken, of course, to say that religion as part of the intermediate area is not challenged. Every claim contains a challenge, be it implied or open. That has always been, and is, an integral, inescapable facet of our earthly religious experience: claims and challenges, claims and challenges, for thousands of years, from rival pagan gods to rival monotheistic creeds, from rival interdenominational sects (Protestant-Catholic, Sunni-Shi'ite, Orthodox-Reformed) to rivalrous religious families calling each other names up and down the streets of their towns and cities. I won't repeat the names. Note this brief passage from a recent article by Leonard George (2000, 7): "in 1950, Pius XII pronounced ex cathedra that the Virgin Mary emigrated to heaven, body and soul, at the end of her life. (He learned this via 'special divine assistance.') Catholics have no wriggle room here. They must believe this dogma, for as Pius put it, 'if anyone, which God forbid, should dare willfully or call in doubt that which We have defined, let him know that he has fallen away completely from the divine and Catholic faith.' " Or this (George 2000, 7): "the Cathars' last redoubt was the mountain fortress of Montsegur, which fell to crusaders in 1244. Although the loss of Montsegur was a bitter blow, three other castles in the region—Puilaurens, Fenouillet, and Queribus—endured for some time as Cathar strongholds. The last to go was Queribus, in 1255. Even then Catharism held on in pockets throughout western Europe. Unable to crush this popular heresy either by debate or crusade, the Catholic church invented another strategy: the Holy Inquisition. The rest, sadly, is history." I, or anyone else, could easily cite a thousand similar passages from the history of the world's religions. The point is, although Winnicott's contributions to our understanding of human behavior are considerable, although his analyses of transitional objects and transitional phenomena assist us hugely in grasping the underlying dynamics of religious conduct, Winnicott was not an esthetician, or an epistemologist, or a historian. He was a brilliant and busy child psychologist. His comments on religion and art, as well as on subjectivity and objectivity, were made in passing. He did not explore the implications of those comments. In the hands of his followers, unfortunately, Winnicott's passing references to art and philosophy are transformed into an obfuscatory, confusional presentation of the religious realm—and just about everything else.

Let's assume for the sake of argument that there is such a thing as reality, as Winnicott (1971, 3) suggests there is; and let's also assume that religion resides somewhere upon a continuum between the subjective and objective poles, as Winnicott (1971, 14, 20) says it does. Surely the question immediately arises, where on the continuum does religion reside? If everything in the "intermediate area" is partly subjective and partly objective, then to what degree is religion subjective and to what degree is it otherwise? As I've just noted, Winnicott never addresses this, and with the exception of Meissner (to whom we'll turn momentarily) neither do his followers. "Winnicott was accurate," writes Rizzuto (1979, 209), "in locating religion—and God—in what he called transitional space. That is the space for illusion, where art, culture, and religion belong. That is the place where man's life finds the full relevance of his objects and meaning for himself. . . . Reality and illusion are not contradictory terms. . . . Men cannot be men without illusion. The type of illusion we select—science, religion, or something else—reveals our personal history and the transitional space each one of us has created between his objects and himself to find 'a resting place' to live in." Instead of sorting out the differences between science and religion, or between religion and art, instead of analyzing the matter and coming to some reasonable conclusion, Rizzuto simply lumps everything together, destroying the possibility of clarification, let alone genuine coherence. Everything is reality and everything is also illusion. Or we can turn it around and beget the same result.

Listen to James W. Jones, who is even more eager than Rizzuto to run with this. "Culture, science, religion, and art are . . . normal extensions of the transitional realm. They develop naturally from the pleasures of this intermediate experience" (Jones 1992, 226). Accordingly, "faith, God representations, and symbols . . . stand at the interface of subjective and objective worlds" (Jones 1991, 41). And then, in a major statement of the thesis, "the infusion of meaning from the inner world into actions and objects in the public sphere and/or the expression of inner-generated truths by means of external physical and verbal forms describes not only children's play with teddy bears and empty boxes but also the creation of symphonies, sculptures, novels, and even scientific theories. . . . In discussing transitional objects, Winnicott is not just talking about 'child's play' but proposing nothing less than a psychoanalytic theory of culture that begins from the interpersonal matrix of infant and parent, moves to the development of creativity through play and the use of transitional objects, and ends with the symphonies of Beethoven, the paintings of Rembrandt, and the theories of Einstein" (Jones 1991, 60–61). In his foreword to Spezzano and Garguilo's anthology of religiously informed psychological essays, *Soul on the Couch*, Jones (1997, x) aggressively dismisses any "strict dichotomy" that anyone might wish to create between the "natural sciences and all other fields," that's right, all other fields. He collapses together the inventions of the human imagination and the interpretations of the scientific realm. For the high-flying Jones, there is no difference, ultimately, between the religious poet penning his revelational verses in a meadow, and the natural scientist painstakingly inducing his conclusions in a laboratory. Once the door of subjectivity is opened, once we admit that our assertions about the universe are invariably touched by our biological and cultural presuppositions, anything goes; any belief about the world is just as good as any other belief; because there is "no unitary definition of rationality," as Jones (1997, x) expresses it, everything is equally rational, or equally irrational, depending on which end of the seesaw one rides. Like Rizzuto, Jones chooses to terminate inquiry, analysis, investigation, at precisely the point where they should commence, namely the fine-grained, discursive point where we attempt to discover the subjective and objective elements in our religious, scientific, and philosophical assertions. Might there be an underlying agenda at work here? Of course there is, and the reader has no doubt already discerned it: if science is no more objective than religion, then to be religious is just as intellectually respectable as to be scientific. Religious claims are just as good as scientific claims. If the scientific world has a mind to challenge our beliefs, well, we can challenge it right back. We can say to science, wait a minute; everything is subjective, and that includes what you are doing too!

As I indicated earlier, Meissner (1984, 181) sees the problem and, unlike Rizzuto and Jones, attempts to resolve it. There is something objective, he claims, about the intermediate realm of illusion in which experiences and objects reside; in fact, that realm comprises an "amalgamation of what is real, material, and objective as it is experienced, penetrated and creatively reshaped by the subjective belief and patterns of meaning attributed to the object by the believer." I prick up my ears. "Real, material, and objective" elements within the world of religious belief and behavior? Is Meissner about to create a watershed in world history as the first person to present verifiable substantiations of supernatural claims? Are Winnicott's passing remarks about to be deepened and confirmed in a rigorous, empirical fashion? I'm afraid not. What Meissner has in mind turns out to be the "tradition" the believer discovers as he participates in his religious culture. "The faith of any human being," he writes (Meissner 1984, 179), "is both received from the religious community of his affiliation and created as a matter of internal and subjective expression." Thus "it represents a realm in which the subjective and objective interpenetrate" (178). Meissner (1984, 181) adduces by way of illustration the following: "the individual Catholic's belief in the real presence of Christ in the Eucharist could hardly be maintained, or at least could be maintained only with extreme difficulty, if participation in the Eucharistic liturgy were not surrounded with a panoply of concrete symbolic expressions of what is basically a highly theological and suprasensory understanding." Clearly, Meissner offers us in support of religion's objectivity the very religious items whose objectivity is in question. The individual isn't fantasizing the supernatural realm, suggests Meissner, because that realm has been described for him by the priest with whom he interacts. God is somehow real because we find Him in the Bible.

The hopelessness of this position is surely apparent. Not only can groups of people (cults) walk around in delusional states, but whole societies can exist in various degrees of madness. Imagine ascribing Meissner's objectivity to the Aztec religious practice of cutting out the hearts of thousands, perhaps millions, of sacrificial victims, mostly children between the ages of six and nine. Once we start according objectivity to culture, we're finished. We are as mentally bankrupt, as mentally vulnerable to nonsense (including moral nonsense), as we are when we suggest that any idea is as good as any other because all ideas contain an ineluctable subjective component. When Rizzuto (1979, 49) asserts in one place that God "is the only relevant object who has not undergone and cannot undergo reality testing, "she is both right and wrong. She is right about the lack of reality testing and she is wrong about God as the only object. A good many relevant objects exist—angels, devils, ghosts—who cannot undergo such testing; indeed, the entire supernatural realm is in exactly this position. That is why religious people are continually seeking for miracles. They are not stupid. They know full well that the only way to establish God's existence beyond question is to establish it within the natural order, verifiably, objectively, empirically, in a manner that is there for all to see.

Religion is based on faith, on the belief in the reality of things unseen. It always has been, and it always will be. Therein lies its distinctiveness;

therefrom arises directly its glorious, timeless power. The semirational, watery approach to religion that we discover in Winnicott's followers is not only mistaken in its basic assumptions, it is destructive of heartfelt, old-fashioned, life-enhancing religious conviction. Religion works best when it involves what Kierkegaard (1941, 208–9) calls "the leap." Compare his views (and his beautiful, vivid sentences) with those of the Winnicottian school. "The wader feels his way with his foot," Kierkegaard writes, "lest he get beyond his depth; and so the shrewd and prudent man feels his way with the understanding in the realm of the probable, and finds God where the probabilities are favorable, and gives thanks on the great holidays of probability, when he has acquired a good livelihood, and there is probability besides for an early advancement; when he has got himself a pretty and attractive wife. . . . To believe against the understanding is something different, and to believe with the understanding cannot be done at all; for he who believes with the understanding speaks only of livelihood and wife and fields and oxen and the like, which things are not the object of faith. Faith *always* gives thanks, is always in peril of life, in this collision of finite and infinite which is precisely a mortal danger for him who is a composite of both. The probable is therefore so little to the taste of the believer that he fears it most of all, since he well knows that when he clings to probabilities it is because he is beginning to lose his faith. Faith has in fact two tasks: to take care in every moment to discover the improbable, the paradox; and then to hold it fast with the passion of inwardness."

This is religion. This is faith. This is what gives us goose bumps whether or not we believe. Once we start talking about meaningful illusions and partial objectivities, once we start working to accommodate religion with science by claiming an affinity through inescapable subjectivity, the game is up. We see too much to come to religion ingenuously as believers, and we see too little to embrace it as passionate, desperate leapers into the paradoxical. As I have suggested in the context of this book, every time the individual prays he asserts through his action itself the anthropomorphic, empathetic reality of his transmundane Creator. Prayer is faith, and faith is manifested chiefly in prayer, because prayer and faith together comprise an elemental commitment to the reality of precisely the unprovable. Religion stops when prayer stops because religion is a living relation with a responsive, supernatural, spiritual being. To be religious is to make the supernatural claim, over and over again, through prayer. To be religious is to challenge oneself, over and over again, upon this sacred, passionate ground. There are no illusions here. There is no intermediate area. It is all, or it is nothing. Those are the alternatives.

For the author of this book it must, of course, be nothing, and the reader knows why. In a recent essay on the origins of prayer in children, Mark Banschick (1998, 85) concedes that supplication is firmly rooted in the infantile period. He then proceeds to point out that a great many human institutions and behaviors are thus rooted, including marriage. "But no one would suggest that marriage is infantile," Banschick concludes. The insuperable problem with this argument from analogy resides in the analogy itself. One marries (let's hope) another human being who is roughly one's equal; not only is one's partner physically existent, or there, one's partner is also capable of responding overtly and immediately to one's overtures and actions. If one is behaving in an infantile fashion, then one can learn all about it, and change. The possibility for a genuinely mature, grown-up marital relationship exists. By contrast, one prays to a supernatural entity through the adoption of a prescribed infantile model, a model which instructs one theologically to assume, as suppliant, the role of a dependent, helpless child (Hallesby [1948] 1979, 20) and to approach the Lord explicitly as an omnipotent, succoring parent, as "a real father" (Heiler [1932] 1997, 98).

Prayer's magical intention is to recapture in idealized form the very infantile relationship upon which one's existence is founded. Psychological regression to infancy is built into the procedure as an essential component of its successful enactment. Unless one regresses radically, unless one rediscovers his infantile bond to the caregiver and transfers it to his current spiritual guide, one falls short of the magical goal toward which he directs his emotions. While one may grow in prayer as one proceeds through life, while one may become, say, less concerned with self and more concerned with others, one is fated to keep both magic and infantile dependency alive as long as one continues to pray to an anthropomorphic parental presence who is lovingly devoted to His child's idiosyncratic wishes and needs. Each and every time one conjures up this arrangement one reinforces the infantile, magical dimension of his character. What is equally important to underscore here, however, is the connection between religion's inescapable infantilism and something we discussed a few paragraphs earlier, namely its historical tradition of persecution and war, its intolerance of dissent, its appetite for violence and terror. Because religion keeps infantilism alive, because through transformational prayer we become magically, emotionally, perceptually God's dependent, helpless children, beholden to Him and to Him primarily for our security and our salvation, those who challenge our God with their alternative claims threaten us, His vulnerable kin, at the elemental, infantile level of our existence. If we worship as infants we will behave as infants in a world of various attitudes and creeds. The other's claim, the other's challenge—whether the other be individual or group—reaches down to our infantile supplicatory roots where our primal anxieties and attachments reside. What looms for us unconsciously in the hated claim and challenge of the other is precisely separation and loss, including of course, and perhaps above all, the final separation of death and the unthinkable loss of our promised immortality.

Is it any wonder that we wish to exterminate the unbeliever? His very existence constitutes an imperfection, a flaw, in our precious, soothing fantasy of ontic security and eternal union. Accordingly, when Rizzuto (1979, 209) tells us that "men cannot be men without illusion," or when Meissner (1992, 182) suggests that "human life becomes impoverished and withers" when the illusory realm is ignored, we soberly reply, maybe so; but that doesn't mean men cannot be men, or thrive as persons, without the religious illusion; indeed, they may have a better chance of growing up and serving well in the absence of this particular consolation.

During the course of a strikingly original lecture presented to the Ernest Becker Foundation in the fall of 1999, Sheldon Solomon (1999) strove to establish the thesis that people gathered together in the world's first towns nine-thousands years ago not to farm, the traditional explanation, but to pray, to huddle spiritually together, to deal with their growing anxiety—including their anxiety over death. What triggered this outbreak of primordial angst among the world's first townspeople? Solomon observed that expanding consciousness, expanding awareness, while evolutionally advantageous in many ways, also harbors a dark side. When people become aware of themselves as people, they also become aware of themselves as objects. Present today, they are gone tomorrow, the foolish and the wise together. Death takes up its place in the developing human mind. The result? People attempted to deny the facts by inventing the gods and the priests and the kings, entities designed to manipulate, to control the powers of life and death. More specifically, they projectively extended to superhuman entities the transference love they experienced for their caring, all-powerful parents. They pacified themselves through their minds by creating culture with its hierarchical authorities and otherworldly illusions. Once pacified, once reassured, once magically restored, they were able to reason their way toward the accomplishments of collective, civilized existence as we usually conceive of it. Solomon's thesis, needless to say, departs radically from established positions among anthropologists and will require considerable amplification before it can compete with the current materialist narrative. However, it is Solomon's concluding extrapolation to our own scientific, psychological age that intrigues me particularly and that can be appreciated entirely upon its own merit, without the need for any thematic, contextual connections.

Having seen into the anxiety-laden ground of our existence as mortal creatures, having stared directly at Yorick's skull and the cultural institutions that spring forth from it, we have only one choice: to grow up, to face reality, to accept the burden of our insight as mature men and women. Yet is it not ironic (and perhaps wonderful) that the tool of insight which destroyed our illusions by revealing them to be the product of our projected transference love is also the tool which discovered the transference love itself! The very instrument, the very psychology, that dispatches God and king and priest is also the instrument, is also the psychology, that discloses discursively and uniquely the vital, all-sustaining nature of parental ministration, authentic, unconditional loving, unconditional caring. Yes, we lose the Almighty and the illusions of the supernatural, we lose the alternative that proved salvational for William James, but we gain in the process a precious insight into our foundation as people. Of course it may not be enough. Of course the thirst for superhuman protectors and assuagers may be unquenchable, and forever so. Still, the transference love that fashioned such beings can be directed inwardly, toward the solitary self, the self that is able through introspection to find the nurturing object within; it can also be directed outwardly from one person to another, from one's self to one's fellow creature, one's companion in the starkness of our condition on the planet. Can we be reaching, through reason informed by empathy, the stage of our history as a form of life in which we come to realize that growing up means loving one another instead of idealized supernaturals and kings? Can the love that sustained us long ago sustain us again demystified? What else *have* we, I wonder, as the kings and supernaturals depart? What's new under the sun?

REFERENCES

Banschick, M. 1998. "The Origins of Prayer in Children." In *The Power of Prayer*, ed. D. Salwak. Novato, Calif.: New World Library, 77–85.

Freud, S. 1964. *The Future of an Illusion*. Trans. J. Strachey. New York: Doubleday.

George, L. 2000. "To Err Is Human, to Forgive Divine." *The Georgia Straight*, June 22, 7.

Hallesby, O. [1948] 1979. *Prayer*. Trans. C. Carlsen. Leicester, England: Intervarsity Press.

Heiler, F. [1932] 1997. *Prayer: A Study in the History and Psychology of Religion*. Oxford: Oneworld Publications.

James, W. [1902] 1987. *The Varieties of Religious Experience*. New York: Library of America.

Jones, J. 1991. *Contemporary Psychoanalysis and Religion*. New Haven: Yale University Press.

Jones, J. 1992. "Knowledge in Transition: Toward Winnicottian Epistemology." *Psychoanalytic Review* 79: 222–37.

Jones, J. 1997. Foreword to *Soul on the Couch: Spirituality, Religion, and Morality in Contemporary Psychoanalysis*, ed. C. Spezzano and G. Gargiulo. Hillsdale, N.J.: The Analytic Press.

Kierkegaard, S. 1941. *Concluding Unscientific Postscript*. Trans. D. Swenson. Princeton: Princeton University Press.

Meissner, W. 1984. *Psychoanalysis and Religious Experience*. New Haven: Yale University Press.

Meissner, W. 1992. "Religious Thinking as Transitional Conceptualization." *Psychoanalytic Review* 79: 175–96.

Polkinghorne, J. 1998. *Belief in God in an Age of Science*. New Haven: Yale University Press.

Rizzuto, A.-M. 1979. *The Birth of the Living God: A Psychoanalytic Study*. Chicago: University of Chicago Press.

Solomon, S. 1999. *Why Settle Down? The Mystery of Communities*. Presented to the Ernest Becker Foundation, Seattle, Wash., September 1999. Available on tape through The Ernest Becker Foundation, 3621 E. 72nd Ave. S.W., Mercer Island, Wash., 98040.

Winnicott, D. 1971. *Playing and Reality*. New York: Basic Books.

Index

About the Author

M. D. FABER is Professor Emeritus of English Language and Literature at the University of Victoria, British Columbia, and a psychoanalytic commentator on religion, philosophy, literature, and art. He has recently published a trilogy on modern religion including the titles *Modern Witchcraft and Psychoanalysis* (1993), *New Age Thinking: A Psychoanalytic Critique* (1996), and *Synchronicity: C. G. Jung, Psychoanalysis, and Religion* (Praeger, 1998).